Washington, D.C. with Kids

Open Road *is* Travel!

OPEN ROAD TRAVEL GUIDES:
THE ONLY WAY TO SEE PLANET EARTH

Whether you're going abroad or planning a trip in the United States, take Open Road along on your journey. Our books have been praised by **Travel & Leisure, The Los Angeles Times, Newsday, Booklist, US News & World Report, Endless Vacation, American Bookseller, Coast to Coast**, and many other magazines and newspapers!

Don't just see the world – experience it with Open Road!

About the Authors

Barbara Pape and Michael Calabrese are a husband-wife writing team who have published in and worked on political, education, and economic issues. They have two children, Anthony and Carravita, whose many tips and suggestions found their way into this book! They are also the authors of Open Road's *Italy With Kids*, and make their home in Chevy Chase, Maryland.

Open Road *is* Travel!

Open Road Publishing has guide books to exciting, fun destinations on four continents. As veteran travelers, our goal is to bring you the best travel guides available anywhere!

No small task, but here's what we offer:

• All Open Road travel guides are written by authors with a distinct, opinionated point of view – not some sterile committee or team of writers. Our authors are experts in the areas covered and are polished writers.

• Our guides are geared to people who want to make their own travel choices. We'll show you how to discover the real destination – not just see some place from a tour bus window.

• We're strong on the basics, but we also provide terrific choices for those looking to get off the beaten path and experience the country or city – not just see it or pass through it.

• We give you the best, but we also tell you about the worst and what to avoid. Nobody should waste their time and money on their hard-earned vacation because of bad or inadequate travel advice.

• Our guides assume nothing. We tell you everything you need to know to have the trip of a lifetime – presented in a fun, literate, nononsense style.

• And, above all, we welcome your input, ideas, and suggestions to help us put out the best travel guides possible.

Washington, D.C. with Kids

Open Road *is* Travel!

Barbara Pape & Michael Calabrese

Open Road Publishing

Open Road Publishing

We offer travel guides to American and foreign locales. Our books tell it like it is, often with an opinionated edge, and our experienced authors always give you all the information you need to have the trip of a lifetime. Write for your free catalog of all our titles.

Open Road Publishing
P.O. Box 284, Cold Spring Harbor, NY 11724
E-mail: Jopenroad@aol.com

2nd Edition

Cover photos by Barbara Pape & Michael Calabrese. Map by Douglas Morris, based on a design by D. Halstead.

The authors have made every effort to be as accurate as possible, but neither they nor the publisher assume responsibility for the services provided by any business listed in this guide; for any errors or omissions; or any loss, damage, or disruptions in your travels for any reason.

Contents

4. Basic Information   48

5. Reading & Web Sites   51

6. Where Are We Going Now?   56

7. Just Outside D.C.   126

8. Field Trips   141

9. I'm Hungry!   154

10. Which One is My Room?   173

Index   183

Washington, D.C. Map 58-59

Washington, D.C. with Kids

Washington, D.C. with Kids

&

1. INTRODUCTION

Washington, D.C., America's capital city, beckons tourists and power brokers alike, with a warm handshake and an invitation to discover how a nation was born and what that nation has done to sustain itself and its people for the past two and one-half centuries.

For children, Washington, D.C., is a living history book. Where else can a child watch the nation's laws being made? Or peek in on the chamber of the all-powerful U.S. Supreme Court? A march from monument to monument gives children and adults alike a taste of the magnitude of the ideas on which America was formed and the price many paid to keep democracy's flame burning.

Alexis de Tocqueville once wrote in 1808 that Washington was "less a city than a grotesque expression of faith and hope." Well, while Washington remains an expression of faith and hope, grotesque or not, it has become a teeming city. Government workers flock to their jobs on and around Capitol Hill. Gucci-clad lobbyists and lawyers, the older ones cruising town in their Jaguars, head for long days at their downtown offices. Lately, a stream of high-tech workers have paved a new path on the Information Highway, one leading straight to Washington, D.C. Washington is a city that works – endlessly.

Politics and power are intoxicating. Front-page headlines blast the latest national scandals. TV shows like West Wing bring to your living room the inner workings of government at the highest levels. Washington, D.C., has endured swamps and malaria, the burning of the White House, presidential assassination, Watergate, presidential weaknesses and terrorist attacks. Yet, every spring the cherry trees bloom their glorious pink buds, the banks of the

Potomac gently lap at the city's shores, massive white-marble monuments glisten in the sun and travelers descend on this city of history.

Washington, D.C., breathes life into history. It is unique. The firebrand revolutionary thought of breaking from Britain to establish a democracy is evident from the halls of Congress to the chambers of the Supreme Court. And, from monument to monument, the challenges that forged modern America – freeing the slaves to saving the world from fascism – are evident.

Washington has moved beyond being the capital city of the United States to being a capital city of the world. Not only in politics, but also in the arts and sciences. Culture and entertainment flourish in Washington. Clustered between Congress and the White House are the Smithsonian museums and the National Gallery of Art— fantastic warehouses of art, history, archeology, paleontology (we're talking lots and lots of dinosaurs) and the wonders of space and space travel from around the world. IMAX theaters have multiplied since we first moved here, showing awesome short films for all ages.

The Kennedy Center, National Theater, Warren Theater, Shakespeare Theater — to name a few — bring top-notch performances to the city on the Potomac. Children's theater, from the Smithsonian's Discovery Theater to Glen Echo's Adventure Theater consistently offer outstanding shows to kids and kids-at-heart.

So, welcome to Washington, a whirlwind city bursting with history, politics and playgrounds.

Chapter 2

OVERVIEW

From Politics to Playgrounds

All roads lead to . . . Washington, D.C. Some descend on Washington to lobby for their cause. Others to seek government grants. A few are elected to represent the folks back home. Still more cling to the winners' coattails in hopes of a job. And, each spring and summer, travelers from all corners of the globe make the journey to see just how America's capital city lives, works and plays.

Look around and you will be shocked to discover that Washington once was nothing more than swamp ground. Embraced by two rivers – the Potomac on one side, the Anascostia on the other – Washington's first settlers were Native Americans, whose artifacts have been found dating back some 6,000 years. The rivers tell the tale of two cities that define Washington.

The Potomac is dramatic, curling 287 miles from just south of Cumberland, Maryland, and crashing through a series of rapids, including Great Falls with a drop of 35 feet. Monuments to American greatness line its banks, including the Jefferson and Lincoln Memorials. The Anacostia is slower-paced, marching to the sea in a short, straight, southwesterly manner. No drama here, just slow and steady. Along its banks are the local neighborhoods –mostly poor and minority – of the native Washingtonians who still lack representation in Congress (the District of Columbia is not a state).

While the high jinx of political life on a national level breathes excitement in this first town of towns, beneath the surface lie the cultural events, parks and playgrounds that grace Washington, creating quite a livable city. The two combine to make it a paradise for traveling with children.

Traveling with Kids

Our first cross-country flight with children was when our oldest was only seven months old. Seasoned travelers – both from business and pleasure – we didn't think twice when we boarded the plane for California. Perhaps we should have thought twice.

On the way over, we had, shall we say, a bit of a diaper emergency. How could this happen? In business class no less. Neighboring passengers were left gasping for breath, and so were we. Flight attendants fluttered over to help the oh-so-obviously inexperienced parents. Where are the diapers? Did we bring any? No, we did not – and neither did we bring any towels or extra blankets, so changing the baby at our seats wasn't an improvement over changing him in the bathroom. Cleaning up with an airplane napkin was our only choice, and of course we did not have another set of clothes handy, either!

Traveling with children requires more advance planning, but it can be equally as enjoying. Many of Washington's sites and monuments are set up to accommodate families traveling with babies – lots of restrooms with changing tables, for instance. And, most of the museums and galleries have renovated to include quite child-friendly, interactive exhibits. Get ready for some fun in America's capital city.

This book includes most of the traditional sites and major attractions in Washington for young and old. Also, it features **Parent Tips** for how to get the most out of sightseeing with children in tow. Our book features special places designed to delight children and their adult companions.

Having children did not quash the lure of travel for us. Over the years, we've learned to adapt (no more dashing through airports to catch the plane just as the boarding gates are closing!) Here are some suggestions for how to get the most out of traveling with children:

Involve Your Children. The more kids participate in the decision-making of the trip the better. Begin to read to them, or suggest for them to read, books and stories about Washington, D.C., American history and national political leaders. Share this travel book with them. The **Fun Facts** are meant just for the kids.

Look at a map, mark your trip and discuss which Washington sites top your list. Is George Washington your favorite? Besides the Washington Monument, you may want to drive out to his splendid home and grounds at Mt. Vernon. Are your children interested in how things are made? Put a checkmark by the Bureau of Engraving, where you will see how money is made. Are dinosaurs a big hit at home? Make sure you go to the National Museum of Natural History on the Mall. Research the American Revolution, colonialism or the Civil War before you visit. Have the kids pick a famous

American political figure – Frederick Douglass or Thomas Jefferson, for example – read about them and design an itinerary that allows the kids to follow their favorite Washingtonian's path

For the very young, get pictures of places in Washington you will be going from your travel agent, travel magazines or on-line. Your child can make a collage of the pictures on poster board, or glue them into a little notebook.

On the Plane or In the Car. For traveling with babies, make sure you have enough extra diapers, a couple changes of clothes, blankets, bottles, toys that distract, something to suck on when the plane takes off and lands – nursing moms, you're it!

Help older children select toys, books and other personal belongings that can fit in their own backpack that they carry. This is key, otherwise you will be schlepping around all the things they cannot carry.

Here are some different ideas of what to put in their packs, all which we used during our many trips to Italy and around and about Washington:

A **walkman and story tapes**. On one trip, our son listened to *The Hobbit* on tape from start to finish.

Coloring books and sketchpads, crayons, markers and watercolor. Children of all ages love to color and draw their own pictures. Try to find coloring books that feature colonial America, a topic relevant to their trip. Watercolor works for older kids. You can get a cup of water anywhere.

Travel version of chess or checkers, preferably a magnetic set.

Sculpty clay. Fun, fun, fun. The kids did everything from designing jewelry to building cities.

Origami. Travel time is a great time to learn this fine art.

Beads. Stringing beads is a pleasant past time for little kids. Keep them in zip-lock bags – the beads, not the kids.

Chapter books. We found that bringing chapter books saved space and weight from bringing individual books even for pre-readers. *Stuart Little* or *Charlotte's Web* can easily be read to younger children with shorter attention spans. You can just stop the story and pick it up later.

Finger puppets. Little children can entertain themselves for some time with a menagerie of little finger puppets.

Puzzles. We carried the pieces in a zip-lock bag. While we didn't use this on the plane or in the car, it's a great idea for a rainy day when you may be locked in a small guestroom with one or more children. We once constructed an entire 1,000-piece rainforest puzzle on a terribly stormy day in Park City, Utah.

Kids Just Want to Have Fun: A tour of the Capitol Building in the morning, hiking around the monuments on the way to lunch on the Mall, with an afternoon jammed packed with dinosaurs, diamonds and dioramas at the Museum of Natural History plus a dash through the Air and Space Museum at the end of the day may sound like a fine itinerary for you but to a child it spells disaster. As our little girl let out after one day like this, "I just want something to climb on!" You will not be able to see everything you want. Visits to the art museum may be shorter, or enjoyed with parents taking turns with the kids. Here are some ideas that work for us:

• Kids like **monuments and sites where they can move around a lot**. In Washington, you have many choices. The Washington, Lincoln, Vietnam, Korean, World War II and FDR memorials are located on lots of land where it is entirely appropriate to romp and play, catch frisbees or even fly a kite. The Jefferson Memorial is on the Tidal Basin where paddleboats come in handy to break up a day of touring. Just remember to spice up your touring with enough outside, active adventures to help kids burn up some energy.

• **Art museums are doable with kids**. Go early in the morning or late in the day to avoid lines and crowds. Bring a sketchbook and pencils or crayons. Most museums allow children to draw and color, as long as they are not running around with the crayons. A group of children from our neighborhood school visit an art museum on days off, led by one of the moms, Milena Kalinovska, who is an art historian. She talks to the children about the art and gives them enough time to sketch and color. Some kids try to copy the masterpieces, others are inspired to draw original work, some scribble. But all of them – from age 4 to 12, including many rambunctious, sports-minded boys – are content to spend at least an hour in an art museum.

• Head right away to the gift shop and buy several postcards of art on exhibit in the museum. Then go on a **treasure hunt in the museum**, where your children will try to find the painting/sculpture on the postcard.

• Many museums in Washington have caught on to the need to make art more interactive for children. We note in this book the museums that provide

Family Packs to make your visit to the art galleries more fun and educational.

- **Play counting games.** Bored in the umpteenth church we entered one day in Italy, our little girl began counting how many candles were burning. She decided to keep a record so she could compare how many were burning in different churches. We had a little extra time to see the church while she busied herself counting all the burning candles! We use this trick wherever we are traveling.

- For older kids, who are critical by nature, ask them to **critique each art museum** they visit, either in a journal, in a hand-held mini-tape recorder or verbally. Was the exhibit interesting? Why or why not? Were there too many pieces of art? What was your favorite painting or sculpture? Why? Modern art museums, like the Hirshorne, can lead to questions of interpretation. Why did the artist choose that color or design? What did he or she mean by their artwork? Does the title match the scene? What would you title the piece?

- Okay, so you try all these nifty ideas and your kids are still staring at you with that "you-must-be-crazy" look. You can: 1. Force them to enjoy art (good luck); 2. Negotiate ("Now if you give us a few minutes of peace here, we'll take you to get ice cream after. . .") that works for awhile; 3. Pass out those game boys; 4. **Give up and split up**. Throughout our book, we try to alert parents to where one of them can go with the kids while the other gets more time in the museum. Sometimes this is simply the best option. Just plan ahead so you know who wants to see what the most. Politics and family living is, after all, the art of compromise.

- **Science Rules.** Go to the library and get a couple of Bill Nye the Science Guy videos to get kids psyched about science, if they're not already. Include the science museums and exhibits when you are traveling in Washington. Our kids, who are fascinated with all things in the cosmos and with inventions, go time and again to Air and Space's How Things Fly and the Science Center at the Museum of American History. The Observatory at Rock Creek Park's Nature Center is great, or, better yet, visit the Science Center in Baltimore.

- **History comes alive in Washington, D.C.** For children who are history buffs, this is a land of sheer delight. Visit your local library before the trip, and save space in your suitcase for extra books you may want to bring back. Let them document their walk through history – from the founding of the nation through The Civil War to modern-day politics — either photographically or by recording it in a journal (see below).

- **Keep a journal**. Kids like to tell their own story and traveling is a great time to keep a record. For pre-readers, they can draw pictures of their trip, with stories dictated to parents. Journals also are a great way for kids to share their travel adventures at school. For our kids, journals were a great way to keep busy while we dealt with the administrative side of traveling – at train stations, long IMAX lines.

- **Give them time to play**. One day on a trip to Italy, we woke up later than our kids to find them quietly playing with little toys they brought along with them. This was week two of our three-week visit. Neither wanted to venture outside for an action-packed day of sightseeing, but preferred to spend the morning playing with their toys. We acquiesced, brought cappuccino and pastries to the room and sat on our hotel balcony to enjoy a quiet moment together.

Chapter 3

PLANNING YOUR TRIP

Climate & Weather

Summer is when most tourists descend on Washington – and it can get hot, real hot, steamy hot and excruciatingly humid. Average temperature during June, July and August is in the 80s, but it can and does get a lot hotter. It's really the humidity that can make it so uncomfortable outdoors. So be prepared with sunscreen, hot-weather clothes, but also sweaters and sweatshirts so you won't freeze in the air-conditioned buildings. You may want to make sure you have a hotel with a pool for an end-of-the-day dip.

Spring and fall are delightful in Washington. If you don't mind your children missing a little school, these are great times to come. The weather is pleasant and tourist attractions not as crowded. Spring is cherry-blossom time and with all the other colorful buds in bloom, Washington looks like a big basket of colored eggs. Fall also is splendid, with the banks of the Potomac bursting with autumn foliage.

Don't hesitate to visit Washington in the winter. Needless to say, it hardly snows and the winters are quite mild. A winter holiday in Washington can be had at a more relaxed pace than in the summer, although there are fewer special events.

We always are amazed when it does snow and the whole city closes down, schools included, due to a sprinkling of snow. Barbara, who hails from Pittsburgh, and Michael, who grew up in Chicago, realize just how much Washington is a southern city when it snows.

What to Pack

We chuckle every time we come to this section in our travel books because packing is just another area in which our habits have changed since traveling with kids. On our bicycle trip through Tuscany before children – a three-week trip – we packed everything we needed in two saddlebags each! Suddenly we're lugging four suitcases with separate carry-on backpacks for the kids and, when our children were younger, a stroller. What went wrong! So here's the advice we obviously have trouble following.

Tip 1: Pack light. Pack your bags once, then go back and remove at least one-third of what you packed. You can always do wash (carry a separate bag to put dirty laundry) or buy extra clothes in Washington. Many hotels have a laundry service, although they are expensive. Take few T-shirts and buy some along the way in Washington. The kids love them as souvenirs.

Tip 2: Bring dress-up clothes only if you plan to attend evening theater performances or know you will go to a fancy restaurant for dinner. Washington is casual, with many fashion critics complaining that it's too casual, with no sense of style. Whatever. Keep the Versace at home. Pull out Gap Kids.

Tip 3: Pack comfortable shoes. This is key because you and your children probably will be doing a lot of walking. Bring at least two pairs.

Tip 4: Make sure you have a light raincoat, preferably with a hood, and at least one umbrella.

Tip 6: Have each child carry a backpack onto the plane or in the car with books, games, coloring materials, walkmen or gameboys, dolls and cuddleys. Pack one change of clothes, toothbrush/toothpaste in the pack just in case you miss a connection. This happened to us once and the kids felt better being able to change. Also, do a last minute check of their backpacks. Our little girl once packed over $20 in coins that her grandma had given her. She struggled carrying this pack through Milan and the Lake region in Italy before we discovered all the money! You never know what they may put in there by themselves.

Tip 7: Give every family member who can handle it (eight and up) their own suitcase on wheels. Older children have their own mid-size suitcase on wheels. Parents carry a larger version of a suitcase on wheels. This way, each person's clothes are separated and no one is carrying too many suitcases by themselves. The kids love the independence and the responsibility and the wheels, they say, make it quite easy to move quickly through an airport or train station.

For ideas of what to pack in the backpack, see the *Traveling with Kids* section in chapter 2.

Strollers & Backpacks

To stroll or not to stroll. Your most difficult decision as you prepare for your trip with a young child/children in tow is how to transport them. We have a novel approach. For children too big for a baby backpack, bring the smallest most compactable jogger stroller. These strollers are tough, durable and light as a feather. We've bounced ours up the steps of the Supreme Court, through the hills of Rock Creek Park and from monument to monument on the Mall. They go where no other stroller has gone before. When our son was younger and too tired to walk, he climbed up on our little girl's lap and off we went. The jogger was put into use as a luggage carrier when we travel through airports and train stations.

For smaller children, a backpack is great for the same reason it is where you live – it's the most portable form of transportation.

Arrivals & Departures

Making Plane Reservations

Booking in advance usually saves you money. Traveling in the off-season (November through April) also is a budget cutter. Unfortunately, the high-season coincides with traditional school breaks, so unless you are willing to take your children out of school, you will be paying top prices. But look out for airline deals.

Once you've decided when you want to travel, there are several ways to check for best prices: You can work with a travel agent, call the carriers yourself, refer to the travel sections in the *New York Times, L.A. Times* or *Toronto Star*, which weekly lists best prices to several destinations, or go surf on the Web. The best websites for comparing prices among many airlines are Microsoft's Expedia (www.expedia.com) and Travelocity (www.travelocity.com). Becoming competitive is Orbitz at www.orbitz.com

Rules vary from airline to airline on children's fares and how to best seat babies and very young children. Check for specifics with either your travel agent or the airline.

Washington has three airports: Baltimore-Washington International (BWI-800/435-9294, www.bwiairport.com) located halfway between Washington and Baltimore; Washington Dulles (703/572-2700), 40 minutes southwest of Washington in Virginia; and, just across the Potomac River from Washington, Reagan National (703/417-8000) in Virginia, but much adjacent to Washington. www.metwashairports.com. National is most convenient to Washington since it has its own Metro stop and is less than a 20-minute drive away.

However, direct flights into National are limited and typically more expensive than flying into Dulles or BWI.

To get from **Dulles** to Washington, you have the following options:

• **Washington Flyer Taxi**, 703/661-6655, one way fares to Washington are about $50.

• **Washington Flyer**, 888/WASHFLY, www.washfly.com, ask for student and group discounts, bus trip to and from Metro's West Falls Church stop, $8 one way, $14 round trip. From there you can take the Metro to Washington.

• **Hotel/Motel Shuttles**, find the hotel/motel shuttle phones in the Baggage Claim area; to meet your shuttle leave the Baggage Claim area down the ramp and out the building to the curbside

• **SuperShuttle,** 800/BLUE-VAN, blue and yellow shared-ride shuttles that will take you to your hotel or most anywhere. SuperShuttle stops are clearly identified on the Ground Transportation Level roadway outside the Main Terminal at Washington Dulles.

To get from **Reagan National** to Washington:

• **Hotel/Motel Shuttles**, find the hotel/motel shuttle phones in the Baggage Claim area; to meet your shuttle leave the Baggage Claim area down the ramp and out the building to the curbside

• **SuperShuttle,** 800/BLUE-VAN, www.supershuttle.com, blue and yellow shared-ride shuttles that will take you to Union Station and elsewhere, SuperShuttle stops are clearly identified on the Ground Transportation Level roadway outside the Main Terminal at Washington Dulles.

• **Taxis,** dispatchers are available at the exits of each airliner to help you find a taxi for Washington, Maryland or Virginia. Cab rides cost about $15 to get to Capitol Hill, $18 to Georgetown.

• **Metro,** 202/637-7000, www.mata.com, the region's rapid transit system stops adjacent to Terminals B and C. Metro fare cards may be purchased from machines at either of two Farecard plazas located on Level 2 near pedestrian bridges that lead into and out of Terminals B and C. A third Farecard plaza for disabled and other passengers using elevators, is under the Metrorail platform, midway between the north and south mezzanines.

To get from **BWI** to Washington:

• **Metro,** 202/637-7000, www.mata.com, BWI just began to run a shuttle from the airport to the Greenbelt Metro stop in November 2001. At 6am the first bus will meet Metro passengers to shuttle them to the airport. From the airport to the Metro, the first bus will leave at 8am. The last bus will leave BWI at 10:50pm. Round-trip fair is $3.15

- **Amtrak or MARC trains,** both Amtrak and MARC, a commuter train service, take BWI passengers to Washington. For more information, call BWI Rail Station (410/672-6167), Amtrak (800/USA-RAIL) or MARC (800/325-RAIL)
- **Taxis,** 410/859-1100, cab fare from BWI to Washington runs about $55.
- **Super Shuttle,** service from BWI runs about 60 minutes after your request (800/BLUE-VAN), rates range from $26 to $32, with $8 charged for each additional rider, children under 6 ride free.

To Washington by Train

Washington is a hub city for Amtrak (800/USA-RAIL, www.Amtrak.com.) Traveling is made convenient by the beautiful and highly efficient Union Station terminal. If you arrive in Washington by train, the Union Station terminal is located right at the foot of Capitol Hill. A cab stand outside makes it incredibly easy to get to your hotel in Washington, or even nearby Maryland or Virginia.

Union Station also is a stop on the Metro (red line). Just travel down the escalator to the Metro station and you can rocket to anyplace the Metro goes.

Our family loves traveling by train. It is so much more relaxing than flying or driving. Amtrak has **discounts for traveling with children**. Kids from 2 to 15 ride half-price when accompanied by an adult, any day and every day. One adult can bring only two children along at this discount. One adult also can bring one child under age 2 for free.

Student discounts also are available. College students can apply for a Student Advantage Card (all information is confirmed with your university). The Student Advantage Card offers 15% off rail fare.

To Washington By Car

During her college days, Barbara was driving from Pittsburgh to Washington, late for a wedding of one of her friends. Everything went smoothly until – the Beltway. Oh, this 66-mile serpent wraps its slithering self tightly around Washington. Cars, trucks, RVs dash wildly around its lanes. Exit signs pop up and disappear within a wink of the eye. One minute you're in Maryland and the next Virginia. Suddenly, Barbara realized that she had seen that exit sign before. It was then she realized – she had circled the entire 66 miles of the Beltway and had missed her exit. Somehow she made it to the wedding before the "I do," but breathless and cursing that darn Beltway.

Ringing the Beltway is more common than you may think. So, here are some hints for beating that snake's tricky tricks. The Capitol Beltway has about 56 interchanges that intersect with every major road leading into Washington. Most of the Beltway is called I-495, but the part leading to Baltimore, Maryland, to the north and Richmond, Virginia, to the south is called I-95.

The trick is not only looking at a map, but knowing which exit to take. A good bet, maybe not the quickest but the easiest, is to get off at the Wisconsin Avenue exit, bear right and follow it all the way to Georgetown. If your hotel is in Dupont Circle or downtown, take Wisconsin to Massachusetts. Make a left on Mass Ave (go just a little beyond the light – there is no right turn at the light – and you will be able to make the right-hand turn) and shoot straight into downtown Washington.

For directions elsewhere, contact your hotel. If you are a member of AAA, request a Trip-Tik before you leave. These are great guides – ones that Barbara began using after her ring around the Beltway.

Public Holidays

Washington is the city that always works!! Thank goodness for these holidays, although the lights may be burning late at night in law offices and lobbyists' suites, most banks, government offices and post offices will be closed. Museums may be open on some of the holidays. Do check under each listing in the *Where Are We Going Now?* chapter for closing days and times.

January 1	New Year's Day
Third Monday In January	Martin Luther King Day
Third Monday In February	President's Day, Washington's Birthday
Last Monday In May	Memorial Day
July 4	Independence Day
First Monday In September	Labor Day
Second Monday In October	Columbus Day
November 11	Veteran's Day/Armistice Day
Last Thursday In November	Thanksgiving
December 25	Christmas

Special Events

January

Martin Luther King Day Third Monday	202/619-7222
Robert E. Lee Birthday January 21	703/548-1789 or 703/557-0613

February

Black History Month	202/357-2700
Frederick Douglass Birthday	202/619-7222
Abraham Lincoln's Birthday	202/619-7222
Chinese New Year Parade	202/789-7000
Revolutionary War Encampment Fort Ward February 17	703/838-4848
George Washington Birthday Parade, Alexandria, Va. mid-February	703/838-4200
Washington Birthday Mt. Vernon mid-February	703/780-2000

March

Women's History Month	202/357-2700
St. Patrick's Day Parade Smithsonian Kite Festival end of March	202/637-2474 202/357-3244
National Cherry Blossom Festival and Parade late March/early April	202/547-1500

April

Easter Egg Roll
White House Lawn
early April   202/456-2200

White House Garden Tour   202/456-2200

Jefferson's Birthday   202/619-7222
mid April

Earth Day Celebrations   202/619-7222
mid April

Shakespeare's Birthday
Folger Library   202/544-4600
late April

Duke Ellington Birthday
late April   202/686-2816

Smithsonian Craft Show
late April   202/357-2700

Georgetown House Tour   202/338-1796

May

Asian Pacific Heritage Month   202/357-2700

National Cathedral Flower Mart   202/537-2937
early May

Georgetown Garden Tour   202/333-3921
early May

Greek Spring Festival   202/829-2910
mid May
Capitol Hill House & Garden Tour   202/543-0425
mid May

Chesapeake Bay Blues Festival
Annapolis
mid May   301/780-5720

Memorial Day Concert
West Lawn/US Capitol
Late May   202/619-7222

Memorial Day
Arlington Cemetery
Late May   202/475-0856

Memorial Day
Vietnam Memorial
Late May   202/619-7222

Memorial Day
U.S. Navy Memorial
Late May   202/737-2300

All Summer Long
Marine Corps Tuesday
Sunset Parades
Iwo Jima Memorial   202/433-4074

Marine Corps Friday Evening
Parades
8th and I Street SE, 8:45pm   202/433-6060

C & O Canal Barge Rides
Georgetown
April through October   202/653-5190

U.S. Navy Band
Capitol, Mondays, 8pm   202/433-6090

U.S. Air Force Band
Capitol, Tuesdays, 8pm   202/767-5658

U.S. Marine Band
Capitol, Wednesday, 8pm   202/433-4011

U.S. Army Band
Capitol, Thursdays, 8pm   202/696-3399

Netherlands Carillon Recitals
Iwo Jim Memorial
Saturdays, 6pm-8pm

U.S. Army Band,
Twilight Tattoo Series
Ellipse, Wednesdays, 7pm   202/685-2851

Washington Cathedral Concerts   202/537-5757

Noon Hour Concerts
Farragut Square, Thursdays   202/619-7222

June
Dupont-Kalorama
Museum Walk Day
Early June   202/939-5568

Garrison Day
Fort Ward, Alexandria
Early June   703/838-4848

African-American
Culture Festival
Late June   202/619-7222

Smithsonian
Festival of American Folklife
Mall, late June   202/357-2700

Capital Jazzfest   301/218-0404

Shakespeare Theatre
Free for All
Carter Baron   202/334-4790

July
D.C. World Jazz Festival   202/783-0360
early July

Independence Day Parade
July 4   202/619-7222

National Symphony and
Fireworks
July 4, 8pm   202/619-7222

Red, White and Blue Concert
Mt. Vernon
July 4   703/780-2000

Bastille Day Waiters' Race
20th and Penn
July 14   202/789-7000
**WHAT A BLAST!!

Festival Latino
Adams Morgan
late July   202/922-0067

Korean War Armistice Day
July 27   202/619-7222

August
Montgomery County, Maryland
Agricultural Fair
early August   301/926-3100

Legg Mason Tennis Classic
mid August   202/721-9500

Arlington County Fair
Arlington, Virginia
mid August   703/920-4556

D.C. Blues Festival
Anacostia Park
late August   202/789-7000

September
Labor Day Weekend Concert
West Lawn, Capitol
early September   202/619-7222

18th-Century Fair
Mount Vernon
early September   703/780-2000

Kalorama House & Embassy Tour
early September   202/387-4062

Rock Creek Park Day
late September   202/387-4062

Annual Croquet Tournament
Ellipse
late September   202/619-7222

October
Hispanic Heritage Month   202/357-2700

Taste of D.C. Festival
early October   202/724-5430

Columbus Day Ceremonies
Union Station
mid-October   202/619-7222

White House Fall Garden Tours
mid-October   202/456-2200

Theodore Roosevelt's Birthday
late October   202/619-7222

Marine Corps Marathon
late October   800/RUN-USMC

November
Veteran's Day Ceremonies
mid November
Arlington National Cemetery   202/475-0843
Mt. Vernon   703/780-2000

December
Holidays at Mt. Vernon
all month   703/780-2000

Festival of Music & Lights
Mormon Temple
all month   301/587-0144

Lighting of
National Christmas Tree   202/619-7222

Old Town Christmas
Candlelight Tours
early December   703/838-4242

White House
Candlelight Tours
mid month   202/456-2200

Getting Around Town

Washington is laid out on a grid, with the Capitol at its center, making it easy (allegedly) to find your way around. From the Capitol, the city is divided into quadrants: **Northeast (NE), Northwest (NW), Southeast (SE)** and **Southwest (SW)**. Please pay attention to the quadrant designations. The same address can be found in all four quadrants! The secret to where you really want to go lies in the quadrant!

Around the Capitol Building you have **North Capitol Street**, which runs north, **South Capitol Street**, runs south, and **East Capitol Street**, which divides the North from the South (no Civil War connection, here). What's missing? West Capitol Street. There is none. West Capitol Street would exist right where there is the National Mall, a large piece of land holding the Smithsonian Museum, National Gallery of Art and monuments. Two major streets embracing the Mall are **Constitution Avenue** to the north and **Independence Avenue** to the south. Ready to move on?

There are lettered streets (C Street SE) and numbered streets (21st Street NW) – don't forget to use those quadrant designations. The lettered streets run east and west and are in alphabetical order. But, there are a few missing ones, like B and J and X, Y and Z. After W Street come one-syllable, two-syllable and three-syllable street names in alphabetical order. Now, isn't that clever? These tend to get you into residential neighborhoods.

Okay, here's where confusion reigns. Avenues with state names — Rhode Island, Connecticut, Wisconsin, to name a few – slice the city diagonally, creating traffic circles and rendering chaos. Round and round you may go on one of these circles, seeking the street you want to end up on. Ooops, past it. Oh no, these other cars careening the circle aren't going to let me get by. Good luck!

Several state-named streets are main arteries throughout the city: **Pennsylvania** (home of the White House) is the avenue of presidential inaugurations and other parades. Pennsylvania Avenue in front of the White House (between 15th and 17th Streets NW) has been closed to traffic for security reasons since 1995.

Connecticut Avenue begins at Lafayette Square, near the White House, and makes its way up, up, up to suburban Maryland, to the Beltway (I-495) and beyond. On the way, you'll pass Dupont Circle and the National Zoo.

Wisconsin Avenue is a main drag through Georgetown. It also continues up through suburban Maryland, where it turns into Rockville Pike.

Along **Massachusetts Avenue** you will find Union Station, Dupont Circle and Embassy Row (look at the flags flying on the front of each embassy and see if you can name that country). Right past the embassies is the U.S. Naval Observatory and vice-presidential mansion. Massachusetts intersects Wisconsin right past the Naval Observatory. One block from the intersection is the National Cathedral. Mass Ave continues to wind all the way through to Maryland. It ends at Goldsboro Road. If you make a left off of Mass Ave. on to Goldsboro, you will come to Glenn Echo Park.

By Car

Driving in Washington is, well, not for the weak of heart. There's morning rush-hour madness, when everyone rockets down the Beltway, Connecticut or Wisconsin Avenues to get to work. Then, there's afternoon rush-hour madness, when all those who aren't total workaholics fly home. Because so many are late-night workers, rush "hour" tends to persist past 7pm. Basically, there are too many people on too few streets and highways.

Parking spaces are endangered species in Washington. Expect not to find a space. Expect to find a space and then be unable to decipher the sign that may be telling you not to park here on Wednesday, but the language is unclear. Expect to have a burning desire to park outside those little white lines that mark the end of official parking on every, single street in Washington. Then, expect to get a big ticket. Expect to feed the meter. Expect to forget to dash out from a museum to feed the meter. Don't play the expectations game. Washington tickets cars agressively. Take the Metro, or walk!

Car Rental

For those of you who choose to ignore our warning up above, you can rent a car at the airport or in several downtown locations. The car-rental companies make it easy for you because so many business conventions are held in Washington. Here's a listing of the main car rental agencies.

• Alamo, www.alamo.com, 800/327-9633
• Avis, www.avis.com, 800/331-1212
• Budget, www.budget.com, 800/527-0700
• Dollar, www.dollar.com, 800/800/4000
• Enterprise, www.enterprise.com, 800/736-8222
• Hertz, www.hertz.com, 800/654-3131
• National, www.nationalcar.com, 800/227-7368
• Thrifty, www.thrifty.com, 800/367-2277

Maps
To help you get around, especially on any road trips to Baltimore, Annapolis, Williamsburg, or elsewhere, here are some good places to pick up maps.

• **ADC Map & Travel Center**, 1636 I Street NW, 202/628-2608, Metro Stop: Farragut North or Farragut West, Open Monday through Thursday from 9am to 6:30pm, Friday from 9am to 5:30pm and Saturday from 11am to 5pm
• **National Geographic Society Store**, 17th and M Streets NW, 202/857-7488, Metro Stop: Farragut North, Open Monday through Saturday from 9am to 5pm and Sunday from 10am to 5pm.
• **Rand McNally Map & Travel Store**, 1201 Connecticut Avenue NW, 202/223-6751, Metro Stop: Farragut North, Open Monday through Friday form 9am to 6:30pm and 7;30pm on Thursday, Saturday from 10am to 6pm.

Another good source is maps found at major bookstores or newsstands throughout Washington. Also, check the local tourist office and your hotel for complimentary maps.

By Metro (www.wmata.com)
This is our preferred way to travel around Washington. It's fast, cheap and cheaper because we don't get parking tickets!! Look out. Washington is keen on pink-ticketing your car. We swear they financed the new convention center on our past tickets alone. We wised up – took us having kids – and now depend a lot more on the Metro.
Here's how the Metro works. Tickets range in price from $1.10 to $3.25, depending on your distance – Metro travels far out into the suburbs. You buy the ticket (Metro pass) at a machine (it takes bills) and slide it into the turnstile to enter. Be sure to keep the tickets, or you will have to pay the maximum price at the other end. You need your ticket to exit the station (you will slide it through another turnstile). The good news is Metro passes are valid basically

forever, not just the day of purchase. Transfers between trains are free; from train to bus is 25 cents. Children under five ride free.

The Metros are marked all around the town by a tall brown column, with a big M and a strip of the color of the line (red, blue, yellow, green, orange). Buy your farecard at the station. Destinations are clearly marked. Flashing floor lights means the train on that side of the track is coming.

The Metro system is open seven-days-a-week. It is open Monday through Thursday from 5:30am to midnight, Friday and Saturday from 8am to 2am and Sunday from 8am to midnight.

However, there is a holiday schedule:

January
New Year's Day (1)   8am to midnight
February
Martin Luther King Day   5:30am to midnight
President's Day   5:30am to midnight
May
Memorial Day   8am to midnight
July
Independence Day (4)   8am to midnight
September
Labor Day   8am to midnight
October
Columbus Day   5:30am to midnight
November
Veteran's Day   5:30am to midnight
Thanksgiving Day   8am to midnight
December
Christmas Day (25)   8am to midnight
New Year's Eve (31)   5:30am to midnight

Parent Tip

The Metro folks recommend that families with strollers use the elevators. Many of the escalators are quite steep. If the elevator is broken, Metro suggests you fold up the stroller and carry the little one in your arms.

By Bus

Metrobus is another way to travel around the city. Bus stops are easily identified across town by their red, white, or blue signs or flags. Look for the route number and destination above the windshield. Metrobus fares run from 50 cents to $2.00, again depending on the distance. Children under five ride free. What fun! On Anthony's sixth birthday, Barbara and he took the bus from National Cathedral down Massachusetts Avenue to Dupont Circle for the first time. When Barbara asked what the fare was for Anthony, the driver asked his age. Barbara told him today is his birthday and he is now six. Not only did Anthony get a free ride, but the entire bus, led by that wonderful Metrobus driver, sang a spirited Happy Birthday to Anthony.

By Taxi

Taxis used to be sooooo cheap in Washington that we never owned a car when we first moved here. Just hailed a cab from point-to-point around town and rented a car for road trips. The historical reason for this, or at least the legendary reason, is that Congress (who still sets the budget for the District of Columbia) did not want to pay high cab fares, so they kept the rates low. They are somewhat more expensive now, but still a great way to move about town.

Typically, it is easy to get a cab downtown and around the Mall and monuments. Just stand on a corner and hail one. There is a cabstand at Union Station. Cabs also congregate around major hotels.

To call a cab, here are the major companies operating in Washington:

- **Capitol Cab**   202/546-2400
- **Diamond Cab** 202/387-6200
- **Red Top Cab**   703/522-3333
- **Yellow Cab**   202/544-1212

If you're in Maryland, call Barwood Taxi at 301/984-1900. We found the drivers to be the most courteous, especially when taking my elderly mother to and from her sundry appointments.

In Washington, taxis charge by the zone (no, this isn't pro basketball, it is legal to use the zone in cab land.) After two decades of living here, we're still not sure where one zone ends and another begins. There is a map in the cab – but it's for people who already know where the zone lines are. Your best bet if you fear getting ripped off is to call Taxi Fare Information (202/331-1671). They know the zone. Give them your beginning and end point, and they will tell you what to expect in the way of a charge. Do remember, there are oh-so-many surcharges: for traveling during rush hour, for each additional passenger after the first, for baggage and if you want to stop on route.

Still, it's not a bad way to move around, especially if you're stay is short. The best deal is cabbing within the single, big Zone One that runs roughly from the Capitol to the White House and encompasses most of the downtown business area.

By Tourmobile
Tourmobile, 202/554-5100, www.tourmobile.com
Bouncing from site to site in these fun red, white and blue tourmobiles is a pleasant way to tour Washington. They provide a powerful overview of the city and its sparkling sites for newcomers and D.C. denizens, alike. The official Tourmobile is run by the National Park Service. They are narrated, often humorous, shuttle tours. Here is a list of ticketbooth locations, although you can also purchase tickets on the tourmobile:

Arlington National Cemetery
June 15 - Labor Day 8:00am-6:30pm
Remainder of the Year 8:00am - 4:30pm
Nearest METRO Stop: Arlington Cemetery

Lincoln Memorial Kiosk
23rd and Independence Ave NW
June 15 - Labor Day 9:30am - 3:30pm
Nearest METRO Stop: Foggy Bottom

White House Pavilion
1501 Pennsylvania Avenue, NW
April - October 9:30am - 2:00pm
Nearest METRO Stop: Farragut West

Washington Monument Kiosk
1401 Jefferson Drive, NW
April - October 9:30am - 3:00pm
Nearest METRO Stop: Smithsonian

Mall - Arts & Industries Building
951 Jefferson Drive, SW
Hours – to be determined (TBD)
Nearest METRO Stop: Smithsonian

Mall - Air & Space Museum
651 Jefferson Drive, NW
Hours - TBD
Nearest METRO Stop: L'Enfant Plaza

Mall - American History
1352 Madison Drive, NW
Hours -TBD
Nearest METRO Stop: Smithsonian

FDR Memorial, West Potomac Park
Ohio Drive, SE
Hours - TBD
Nearest METRO Stop: None

Union Station
49 Massachusetts Avenue, SE
Hours - 9am - 3pm
Nearest METRO Stop: Union Station

Design your own, customized tour. The Tourmobile stops at 25 locations on and around the Mall, Pennsylvania Avenue and Arlington National Cemetery. You can get off one Tourmobile, tour the site at your pace and then board another Tourmobile. (Shhh! Here's a little secret about purchasing tickets. If you buy your ticket after 2:30pm, it remains good for the next day. Check with your driver for details and to ensure that the policy has continued). Here's what you have to choose from:

Arlington Cemetery
Kennedy gravesites
Tomb of the Unknowns
Arlington House
Kennedy Center
Lincoln, Vietnam and
    Korean War Memorials
White House
Washington Monument
Smithsonian Castle and
    Arts & Industries Building
Air and Space Museum
U.S. Botanic Gardens
Union Station and Postal Museum

U.S. Capitol, Library of Congress
    and Supreme Court

National Gallery of Art
Museum of Natural History
Museum of American History
Bureau of Engraving and
    Holocaust Museum
Jefferson Memorial
FDR Memorial
Old Post Office Pavilion
Ford's Theater and FBI Building
National Archives and
    U.S. Navy Memorial
National Law Enforcement
    Memorial
National Museum of American
    Art, National Portrait Gallery
    and MCI Center

The Tourmobile offers its own tours. You can purchase tickets for any of these tours from the Tourmobile drivers, from the Tourmobile kiosks noted above or by calling TicketMaster at 800/551-SEAT. Here are the special tours offered by Tourmobile:

Arlington Cemetery, one and a half to two hour tour, daily except Christmas Day, Hours: 8:30am to 6:30pm April through September, 9:30 to 4:30 October through March, Admission: adults $5.25, children 3-11 $2.25, children under 3 free, Departure: Arlington National Cemetery Visitors' Center only. We found this to be the best way to see Arlington Cemetery. Just remember to bring lots of water if it is a hot, humid day.

American Heritage Tour, full-day tour, operates daily except Christmas day, Hours: 9am to 6:30pm June 15 through Labor Day, 9:30am to 4:30pm rest of year, Admission: adults $18, children 3-11 $8, under 3 free of charge, free re-boarding, with final re-boarding one hour before closing, Departures: from any of their stops (see above).

George Washington's Mt. Vernon: Estate and Garden Tours, four-hour tour, operates daily April through October, Hours: departs 10am, noon and 2pm from the Washington Monument and Arlington Cemetery Visitors' Center stops, Admission: (includes price of admission for Mt. Vernon) adults $25, children 3-11 $12, children under 3 free.

Frederick Douglass Historic Site, three-hour tour, operates June 15 through Labor Day, Hours: departs at noon from the Washington Monument and Arlington Cemetery Visitors' Center stops, Admission: adults $7, children 3-11 $3.50, under 3 free.

Old Town Trolley Tours, 202/832-9800, www.oldtowntrolley.com/ Washington. Another option for touring the city. Old Town Trolley Tours operate from 9am to 5pm daily, closed Thanksgiving and Christmas. Reservations are not required. Trolley Tickets purchased online do not expire and can be used any day. Patrons can present tickets and board at any Old Town Trolley boarding location. The tour lasts about 2 hours and 15 minutes.

Location/Stops are: Union Station, Capitol Arboretum, Old Post Office, China Town, FBI Building/Ford's Theatre, Freedom Plaza/National Aquarium, White House, Lafayette Park, National Geographic Society, Dupont Circle Neighborhood, Kalorama/Adams Morgan, National Cathedral, Georgetown, Lincoln Memorial Complex/Arlingotn Cemetery, Smithsonian West/Holocaust Museum, Air and Space Museum, U.S. Capitol/Library of Congress

DC Ducks, 202/832-9800, www.dcducks.com
This is a blast for kids. The same vehicle travels on sea and land. The "Captain" is a wise-quacking tour guide. It is a 90-minute tour, operating from 10am to 3pm in the summer and spring. Admission: Adults - $25 / Children(4-12) - $13. Boarding Location: Union Station. Notes: Tours depart once an hour - on the hour. Reservations not required. Tour is subject to change without notice due to weather conditions. For departure verification call 202/966-3825. Tickets purchased online do not expire and can be used any day.

By Bike
Bike the Sites, 202/966-8862, www.bikethesites.com
Since the children were off training wheels, we have biked around the

monuments – a fast and fun way to enjoy the Mall. There is a company – Bike the Sites, Inc. – which arranges bike tours for you. Run by a husband and wife team, Lisa and Gary Oelsner, you can arrange one of several tours for you and your family: The Capitol Sites Tour (two and 1/2-hour guided-tour covering eight miles) costs $35 for adults and $30 for children under 13. For that price you get bikes, helmets, water bottle and snack, plus your guide.

There are other tours: Mt. Vernon Tour, Civil War Statues Tour, Bridges Tour and Early Washington Tour. There's even a nighttime tour. Prices vary.

We have not yet tried Bike the Sites. So let us know how it works for you. Or, we'll see you on the trail since we just put in our reservation.

River Cruises

Always a hit with children is a boat trip – in Washington it's a river cruise up and down the Potomac. Below are several options you have to enjoy the sites while sailing the Potomac.

Parent Tip

The dinner cruises, about 3 hours in length, may not be the best for younger children. "Mommy, I'm bored . . . tired . . . scared. . . or seasick," is a problem. You can't get off! There is nowhere to go!! Try the shorter, sightseeing trips first.

$\approx$

Capitol River Cruises (from Washington Harbor, Georgetown), 301/460-7447, www.capitolrivercruises.com, leaves 11am to 9pm on the hour, $10 for adults, $5 for children 3-12, 50 minutes, cruise the Potomac and see the Washington Monument, Jefferson and Lincoln Memorials, Key Bridge, Roosevelt Island and much more.

Cruise Ship Dandy (from Old Town Alexandria), 703/683-6076, lunch cruise: $33 adults, $23 children; dinner: $67.50 adults, $57.50 children (note the $10 discount for children does not apply for Friday or Saturday night), sail under low-arched bridges and see the monuments, Watergate, Kennedy Center and more. Call for schedule.

In Washington for the Fourth of July? See the fireworks from the Dandy!

Odyssey Cruises (from SW Washington), 202/488-6000, www.odysseycruises.com, weekend brunch cruises (11:30am – boards at 10:45 am to 1:30pm), $50.00; Monday through Friday lunch cruise, $38.00 per person, children 3-11 are half price, under 3 free, dinner cruise (3 hours) $80-$90 (8pm to 11pm). Check website for special deals.

Potomac Riverboat (Old Town Alexandria and Georgetown), 703/548-9000, www.potomacriverboatco.com , now running tours seven days a week. Call for schedule, or visit the website. The primary tour is a narrated water taxi that runs between Alexandria, Virginia, and Georgetown. You will pass the monuments, Alexandria Harbor, Georgetown, Kennedy Center and more. There also is a Mt. Vernon Cruise.

Shore Shot Cruises (Washington Harbor, Georgetown), 202/554-6500, www.shoreshot.com, adults $10, children $5 age 4-12, under 4 free, tours offered every day from May 1 through September 29, weekends only from April 13 through April 30 and October 1 through October 13.

Spirit Cruises (SW Washington), 202/554-8000, www.spiritcruises.com, lunch: adults $29.95-$38, $27.95 for children 3-12 (higher during summer months); dinner: $53-$68, $51 for children 3-12 (higher during summer months); this is a huge feast plus cabaret-style entertainment during a two- to three-hour cruise of the Potomac. There also is a narrated tour to Mt. Vernon, with a stop at the grounds and mansion: adults $30.95,children $20.95 age 6-11.

Neighborhoods

Here are just a few of the neighborhoods you can enjoy while visiting Washington.

Capitol Hill

"I work on the Hill," you may overhear someone say. "What hill?" you may wonder. Unless you are from Nebraska, Washington looks pretty darn flat. "And, what do they do on that hill?" Jack and Jill rhymes aside, the Hill is what D.C. denizens call Capitol Hill. Working on the Hill probably means they work for a U.S. Representative or Senator, or maybe the Supreme Court.

The Hill, once called Jenkins Hill, is more than the magnificent Capitol grounds. It extends into charming 19th-century neighborhoods of varied architectural styles. On a walk through the residential areas, you will note examples of Federal, Queen Anne, Italiante and Beaux-Arts architecture. Walk around the side streets directly behind the Supreme Court. But do be careful after dark. The neighborhoods surrounding Capitol Hill have some of the city's highest crime rates.

Capitol Hill is a vibrant neighborhood, with its famous Eastern Market (7th & C Streets SE , Hours: Tuesday through Saturday 7am- 6pm and Sunday 9am -4pm, closed Mondays, Metro: Eastern Market) a bustling 19th-century food emporium. Ohh, the cheeses. Luscious fresh fruit. Smell the baked goods and sniff the gorgeous flowers.

The Mall

Not a shopping mall, but the National Mall. The wide expanse runs from Capitol Hill to the Lincoln Memorial. Within its reach are the Smithsonian Museums, the National Gallery of Art, Botanic Gardens, Washington Monument, Lincoln and Jefferson Memorials, Vietnam and Korean memorials – whew – there's a lot more.

You will spend a lot of time at the Mall. Enjoy!

Downtown

History meets modern office space in downtown D.C. The area extends from K Street to Constitution Avenue and from 15th through 2nd Street – all in the northwest quadrant. Downtown is the home of the White House and the Convention Center - the historic Treasury Building to the MCI Center. In between are law offices, the Shakespeare, Warner and National theaters and much more. The downtown area has become a lot more interesting for kids since the Spy Museum opened. Check out the James Bond car and other spy toys.

Try a walking tour of the downtown area:

Hometown At War: Civil War Washington, 202/828-WALK, Saturday and Sundays April through October at 12:30pm, Meet: At the Gallery Place/Chinatown Metro Station at 7th and F Streets, tours end at Ford's Theatre, Admission: $10 per person.

Discover Historic Downtown DC-A DC Heritage Tour, 202/828-Walk, Saturdays at 2:30pm, Meet: On the corner of 7th and F Streets at the Gallery Place/Chinatown Metro, Admission: $10 per person. Highlights include seeing where Harriet Beecher Stowe found a publisher for Uncle Tom's Cabin, the publication that contributed to the beginning of the war between the North and the South.

Dupont Circle/Kalarama

One of our favorite parts of Washington – where we've both lived and work. Dupont Circle is a vibrant neighborhood, filled with art galleries, restaurants, bookstores and some splendid, small-scale museums (Phillips Museum and Textile Museum, to name two).

The Circle itself is a melting pot of residents, office workers, bicyclists, chess players (there are stone chess tables in the Circle) and travelers. Daniel Chester Finch, the same man who designed the Lincoln Memorial, designed the white-marble Dupont Memorial Fountain. It's hard to believe this urban enclave was once a rural backwater.

Foggy Bottom

Nestled between Lafayette Square and Georgetown is Foggy Bottom, famous for housing the State Department, the World Bank and other international agencies. Here you'll also find the illustrious Kennedy Center, George Washington University and other historic homes and sites. It once was an industrial center for the burgeoning 18th-century Washington.

Georgetown

Shop, shop, shop. Home to Georgetown University and, shops. A neighborhood desired by the rich and famous, and for those who want to shop. Georgetown emerged as a tobacco port on the banks of the Potomac River in 1751. It had several swan songs as a neighborhood, but has emerged as a town within a city.

Georgetown runs from Georgetown University to 23rd Street NW, from the Whitehurst Freeway to the Oak Hill Cemetery. Stunning mansions, brick row houses and lovely gardens grace the charming neighborhood.

Come here to stroll the streets, enjoy dinner, and, in case you forgot, shop.

Playgrounds, Parks, & Recreation

Here are some of our favorite playgrounds:

Parks Aztec Gardens, 201 18th Street, situated between the Organization of the American States and Art Museum of the Americas, open Tuesday through Saturday from 10am to 5pm.

Xochipili, Aztec god of flowers smiles gently on this lovely urban garden, with reflecting pool and sculptures by Latin American artists.

Candy Cane Playground, Rock Creek Park at intersection of Beech Drive and Connecticut Avenue, on the border of Washington, D.C. and Maryland. Swings and things. Great fun, crowded on weekends.

C&O Canal National Historic Park, MacArthur Blvd and Falls Road, Potomac, Maryland, 301/299-3613, open daily from sunrise to sunset, admission: $4 per car, $2 for walk-ins and bikers.

Canal boat rides, footbridges to the Olmsted Island overlook and the Great Falls Tavern Museum. The Park Ranger staff also conduct special programs, including hiking and bird watching. Be careful: The water is dangerous

Dumbarton Oaks, 1703 32nd Street NW, 202/339-6401, www.doaks.org, admission: $4 adults, $3 children under 12.

East Potomac Park (Hanes Point), Ohio Drive SW, near the Tidal Basin, open dawn-dark

Picnic grounds, playground, tennis (202/554-5962) and golf course (202/554-7660). The park also features the remarkable sculpture The Awakening bursting out of the ground and is on the banks of the Potomac River.

Glenn Echo, MacArthur Boulevard at Goldsboro Road

While waiting for an Adventure Theater or Puppet Company production to begin, take a fantasy ride on the Dentzel Carousal, or climb and swing on the playground.

Hanes Point (see East Potomac Park)

Montrose Park, R Street NW, between 30th and 31st Streets, next to Dumbarton Oaks, open dawn to dusk.

Gorgeous, neighborhood park and playground. It also has tennis courts and – smooch, smooch, kiss, kiss – a Lover's Lane.

National Arboretum, 3501 New York Avenue NE, 202/245-2726, www.ars-grin.gov/na , open daily 8am to 5pm, Admission: free.

How exciting can plants be? Quite exciting at this 444-acre arboretum. And, it is soooo child friendly. Right outside the Visitor's Center are koi – huge Japanese carp measuring nearly 3 feet in length. Breathtaking are the 22 34-foot-tall sandstone Corinthian columns that once graced the east portico of the Capitol. A nine-mile drive circles the arboretum – we got out often to look at the beautiful gardens, sculpted bushes, and the ancient National Bonsai Collection (a gift from Japan, the Bonsai are over 300 years old). There also is a 40-minute guided tram tour.

Rock Creek Park, through the city, 202/282-1063, open dawn to dusk.

Hikes, bikes, horses, tennis and boating. It's all about nature and a great retreat from the hustle-bustle of Washington.

Theodore Roosevelt Island, Potomac River near Georgetown, off George Washington Memorial Parkway, between Key and Roosevelt bridges, 703/285-2598, open dawn to dusk.

Hike along the nature trails on this 88-acre island. Once, Native Americans inhabited this land, which now is dedicated to Roosevelt's conservation efforts. We sometimes bike here from the Rock Creek Park bike path. Warning: Look out for the mosquitoes.

Biking

Biking is the best in Washington – so many paths. Trails include: Capital Crescent Trail, between Georgetown and Bethesda, Maryland; Rock Creek Park, from Watergate past the zoo and along Beach Drive to Maryland; George Washington Memorial Parkway, from Memorial Bridge through downtown Alexandria, Virginia, and ending at Mt. Vernon; and the C&O Canal Towpath, a 23-mile trail from Georgetown to Seneca, Maryland.

Call the **Washington Area Bicyclist Association** for more information at 202/872-9830.

Hiking

Best bets are Rock Creek Park, C&O Canal, Theodore Roosevelt Island and the U.S. National Arboretum. A favorite of children from our neighborhood is the nearby Billy Goal Trail in Potomac, Maryland (301/299-3613).

Horseback Riding

Rock Creek Horse Center (202/362-0117) for 11 miles of bridle trails.

Music

Blues Alley, 1073 Wisconsin Avenue NW, 202/337-4141, jazz

Dubliner, 520 North Capitol Street NW, 202/737-3773, Irish
Zanzibar, 700 Water Street SW, 202/667-5370, jazz, blues, Caribbean

Nature Center

Audubon Naturalist Society (Woodend), 8940 Jones Mill Road, Chevy Chase, 301/652-9188, www.audubonnaturalist.org, Admission: free.
Our children adore the Audubon society. They explore the self-guided nature trails, have taken classes there and particularly enjoy the pond at the end of the trail. We have spent many a spring day, stretched out at the pond, searching for toads, sketching the woods and just daydreaming.

Sports Events

DC Armory/RFK Stadium, 20010 East Capitol Street, 202/547-9077
FedEx Field, Redskin Road, Landover, Maryland, 301/276-6050 (home of the NFL Redskins)
MCI Center, 601 F Street NW, 202/628-3200 (home of the NBA Wizards and the NHL Capitals)
Oriole Park at Camden Yards, Baltimore, Maryland, 410/685-9800 (home of the American League Orioles)

Tennis

Rock Creek Park courts are located at 16th and Kennedy Streets NW, north of the National Zoo. Reserve courts form April to November by calling 202/722-5949. Or, reserve time at **East Potomac Park**, 1090 Ohio Drive SW by calling 202/554-5962 (near the Tidal Basin and Jefferson Memorial). There are 24 courts (indoor, outdoor, lighted and clay), open spring through fall from 7am to 8pm.

Theaters

Arena Stage, 6th and Maine Avenue SW, 202/488-3300
Carter Barron Amphitheater, 4800 Colorado Avenue NW, 202/426-6837
Center for the Arts, George Mason University, Fairfax, Virginia, 703/993-8888
DAR Constitution Hall, 1776 D Street NW, 202/628-4780
Ford's Theater, 511 10th Street NW, 202/347-4833
John F. Kennedy Center, 2700 F Street NW, 202/467-4600
  American Film Institute, 202/785-4601
  Concert Hall, 202/467-4600
  Eisenhower Theater, 202/467-4600
  Opera House, 202/467-4600
  Terrace Theater, 202/467-4600

Theater Lab, 202/467-4600
Lincoln Theater, 1215 U Street NW, 202/328-6000
Lisner Auditorium, 730 21st Street NW, 202/994-1500
Merriweather Post Pavilion, Columbia, Maryland, 301/982-1800
National Theater, 1321 Pennsylvania Avenue NW, 202/628-6161
Shakespeare Theater, 450 7th Street NW, 202/547-1122
Signature Theater, 3806 South Four Mile Run, Arlington, Virginia, 703/
820-9771
Source Theater, 1835 14th Street NW, 202/462-1073
Warner Theater, 13th Street between E and F Street NW, 202/628-1818
Wolf Trap, 1624 Trap Road, Vienna, Virginia, 703/255-1868
Wooly Mammoth, 1401 Church Street NW, 202/393-3939

Symphony/Ballet/Opera
National Symphony, 202/467-4600
Washington Ballet, 202/467-4600
Washington Opera, 202/295-2420
Washington Chamber Orchestra, 202/452-1321

Tickets
ASC Tickets, 800/786-8425, www.ascticket.com
Executive Tickets, 800/637-3719, www.exectick.com
Great Seats, 877-478-SEAT, www.greatseats.com
Tickets.com, 703/218-6500
Ticketmaster, 202/432-SEAT, www.ticketmaster.com
TICKETPlace, Old Post Office Pavilion, 1100 Penn Avenue NW, 202/842-
5387 (half-price tickets, day of show)

WaterSports
Rent a small boat or canoe from Fletcher's (202/244-0461) or Thompson's (202/333-4861) Boat Houses.

Canal boat rides also are available. The Georgetown is docked on the canal between 30th Street and Thomas Jefferson Street NW in Georgetown (202/653-5844. Or try the Canal Clipper (301/299-2026), which departs from Great Falls in Potomac, Maryland.

Chapter 4

BASIC INFORMATION

Hospitals
The hospitals in Washington are well reputed worldwide.
- **Children's Hospital,** 111 Michigan Avenue NW, 202/884-5000
- **Columbia Hospital for Women,** 2425 L Street NW, 202/293-6500
- **George Washington University Hospital,** 901 23rd Street NW, 202/994-1000
- **Georgetown University Hospital,** 3800 Reservoir Road NW, 202/687-2000
- **Howard University Hospital,** 2041 Georgia Avenue NW, 202/865-6100
- **Sibley Memorial,** 5255 Loughboro Road NW, 202/537-4000
- **Washington Hospital Center,** 110 Irving Street NW, 202/877-7000

24-Hour Pharmacy
- **CVS** in Dupont Circle, 202/833-5704
- **CVS** in Bethesda, 301/656-2522

Police
Dial 911 or 311

Safety & Security
Stating that security at airports and around Washington has been beefed up since September 11 is noting the obvious. From more police on the streets to high-tech sensors for biological weapons and radioactive material, Wash-

ington is pushing forward to making the city as safe as it can. While no one can make sweeping claims for the safety of Washington, or any other city, here are some of the things you can expect to see and not to see.

There are more police and police dogs roaming the Metro. By the time you have this book, there may be monitors at each and every monument and on the Mall. The Federal Transportation Security Administration has taken over security at airports beginning in February 2002.

As a traveler to Washington, what does all of this mean for you? That you are probably safer now than before 9-11, but as with every town and village across the world, there is no guarantee.

Some tips offered by airport security personnel: Don't joke around at security points at the airport or anywhere else. Security is serious business. They also suggest that at airports you come prepared to have your luggage or yourself searched and expect to be delayed. Come with a good attitude! Cooperation is essential. Check in at least two hours early and bring a photo ID, not only to the airport, but for bus and train rides, too. Do not bring toy guns, darts, knitting needles or crotchet hooks.

Washington is a big city and like any other big city there is crime, although quite a bit less than a decade ago. Some street-smart tips:

• If you like, wear a money belt.
• Make sure your backpack is zipped and be aware of it when you are in crowded places like the subway.
• Don't walk in isolated places.
• Keep your children within sight.

Washington D.C. Fun Facts

• Washington, D.C., by many is considered part of the South, located just north of Virginia and south of Maryland
• It is only 68 square miles.
• Washington, D.C.'s, state bird is the wood thrush.
• Its flag is white with three red stars and two horizontal red stripes.
• The major industries of Washington are the federal government and, did you guess? tourism!
• Washington's motto is *Justitia Omnibus,* or Justice For All.
• The city's flower is the American Beauty Rose.
• Washington, D.C., is nestled between two rivers: The Potomac and the Anacostia.
• Algonquian-speaking tribes once inhabited the land, including the Iroquioan, Siouan, the Conoys and the Patawomeke.
• In 1942, the leg bone of a brachiosaurid was dug up near what is now the Shrine of the Immaculate Conception.

☙

Play it safe and you'll enjoy your trip to Washington.

Time

Washington, D.C., operates on Eastern Standard Time.

Info & Help

• **Travelers Aid,** 301/773-6361

• **Washington Convention & Visitor Association,** 1212 New York Avenue NW, Suite 600, Washington, D.C. 20005, 202/789-7000, Fax 202/789-7037, www.washington.org

Chapter 5

READING LISTS & WEB SITES

No true adventure begins without a handful of stories to wet one's appetite for the excitement in store for young – and older – travelers. So many fascinating people and much of America's history reside in Washington. We hope your family enjoys these books about Washington and the Washingtonians.

Children's Books

Colonial Days and the American Revolution

Meltzer, Milton. *The American Revolutionaries: A History in Their Own Words 1750-1800.* (1987). Thomas Y. Crowell, New York. Uses historical letters, diaries, journals, interviews, ballads, newspaper and more to document the life and times of ordinary and extraordinary men, women and children living through the American Revolution.Middle school to high school – or read-aloud to upper-elementary students.

Smith, Carter (editor). *The Revolutionary War: A Sourcebook on Colonial America.* (1991). Milbrook Press Inc.Packed with facts, reproductions of key documents and lots of illustrations. The text is broken up to make it more readable. Wonderful thumb-nail sketches of the life and times of the Revolutionary War. Upper-elementary through high school.

Day, Nancy. *Colonial America.* (2001). Runestone Press.

January, Brendan. *Colonial Life.* (1972). Children's Press.

Moore, Kay. *If You Lived at the Time of the American Revolution.* (1997). Scholastic Inc.

Forbes, Esther. *Johnny Tremain.* (1944) Yearling Books. Newbery Winner.

A favorite of Anthony's about a young, disabled silversmith who overcomes adversity to find success during the early dawn of the American Revolution.

Fritz, Jean. *And Then What Happened, Paul Revere?*. (1998) Putnam. Or any of Fritz's delightful books on early Americans and American history.

Latham, Jean Lee, *Carry on Mr. Bowditch*. (2003). Houghton Mifflin. One of Carravita's favorite books of this time period, written about the mathematician and navigator Nathaniel Bowditch.

Civil War

Bakeless, Katherine and John. *Confederate Spy Stories*. (1973). J.B. Lippincott Company. Short chapters, historic spy stories written to thrill readers with daring stories of Confederate spies.

Clinton, Catherine. *Encyclopedia of the Civil War*. (1999). Scholastic Inc. More than just the facts, this encyclopedia includes Battles at-a-Glance inserts, interesting sidebars (for example, "Children and the Military" discusses "powder monkeys," children who worked on gunships. Learn more about powder monkeys in this book's section on Baltimore.

Haskins, Jim. *Black, Blue and Gray: African Americans in the Civil War*. (1998). Simon and Schuster. Meet African Americans who fought long and hard during the Civil War, yet are often forgotten in school textbooks. Upper elementary and above.

Herbert, Janis. *Civil War for Kids*. (1999). Chicago Review Press. History combined with 21 activities. Elementary school.

Mettger, Zak. *Till Victory is Won: Black Soldiers in the Civil War*. (1994). Lodestar Books. Based on many first-person accounts, this book reveals the story of how both free and enslaved black men we recruited, fought, died and influenced the outcome of America post Civil War. Wonderful vintage photographs. Upper elementary and above.

Ray, Delia. *A Nation Torn. (1990)*. Lodestar Books. The roots and causes of the Civil War, as well as battles won and lost, are described in this book through the eyes of people living, working and going to war in the mid-1800s. Elementary school.

Polacco, Patricia. *Pink and Say*. (1994). Philomel Press. Beautifully written and illustrated story of interracial friendship during the Civil War. Polacco is a critically acclaimed children's author. Elementary and above.

Day, Nancy. *Civil War*. (2001). Runestone Press.

America & Americans

Bennett, William (editor), *The Children's Book of America*. (1998). Simon and Schuster. Written by the author of *The Book of Virtues,* this book shows how virtues such as compassion, perseverance, ingenuity and hard work formed America and shaped its history. Elementary school.

Ferris, Jeri. *What Are You Figuring Now? A Story about Benjamin Banneker.* (1988*).* Carolrhoda Books, Creative Minds Series.

Kroll, Steven. *By the Dawn's Early Light: The Story of the Star-Spangled Banner.* (1994). Scholastic. Beautiful illustrations and interesting story on the origin of the *Star-Spangled Banner.* Elementary and above.

Grant deParuro, Linda. *Founding Mothers: Women in America in the Revolutionary Era.* (1975). Houghton Mifflin. Thought women were non-existent during Revolutionary times? Think again. Advanced middle school, high school.

Meltzer, Milton (editor), *Frederick Douglass: In His Own Words.* (1995). Harcourt Brace (Parent's Choice Award). Look for these other books by Meltzer on famous Americans, including Lincoln, Thomas Jefferson, George Washington, Theodore Roosevelt, Andrew Jackson and Benjamin Franklin. Middle school and up.

Presidents

Bausum, Ann, (with forward by George W. Bush). *Our Country's Presidents.* (2001). National Geographic.

Provensen, Alice. *The Buck Stops Here: The Presidents of the United States.* (1990). Harper and Row. Each president gets a page, with illustrations that tell more of their story than the poem that connects one president with another. There are more extensive notes on each president at the end. The last president covered is George Bush Sr., the 41st.

St. George, Judith and Small, David. *So You Want to be President?* (2000). Philomel Press. Caldecott winner.

Turner, Ann. *Abe Lincoln Remembers.* (2001). Harper Collins. Elementary school.

Winnick, Karen. *Mr. Lincoln's Whiskers.* (1996). Boyds Mill Press. Elementary school.

The White House

Harness, Cheryl. *Ghosts of the White House.* (1998). Simon and Schuster. In a Magic School Bus format, Sara is plucked away from her school's White House tour by the ghost of George Washington, who then gives his own tour of the White House where she meets the ghosts of past presidents. Elementary school and up.

Kay, Kathleen. *It Happened in the White House.* (2000). Hyperin Press.

Waters, Kay. *The Story of The Whit House.* (1991). Scholastic. As easy-read tour of the White House, with lots of fun facts. Elementary.

Washington, D.C.: America's Capital City

Hoig, Stan. *A Capital for the Nation*. (1990). Cobblehill Books. Doing a school project on Washington? This book gives all the details and more. Middle school and up.

Means, Howard and Llewellyn, Robert. *Washington: The District and Beyond*. (1989). Howell Press. Aerial photography of Washington, with text. Great photos. All ages.

Munro, Roxie. *The Inside-Outside Book of Washington, D.C.* (1987). E.P. Dutton. Full-page illustration of places to see in Washington, D.C. Early elementary.

Reynolds, Patrick. *A Cartoon History of The District of Columbia*. (1997). That's right: a cartoon-style history of Washington.

Stein, Conrad R. *Washington, D.C.* (1999). Children's Press. A good tour of Washington, from its early days to current attractions. Upper elementary and above.

Williamsburg

Anderson, Joan. *A Williamsburg Household*. (1988). Houghton Mifflin. A comparison of the lives of slaves and their owners, in story form. Elementary.

Kassem, Lou. *A Haunting in Williamsburg*. (1990). Avon Camelot. Picked this up at the school book fair. Good "beach" reading. Upper elementary and above.

Series

"Cornerstones of Freedom" series covers sundry issues and places about America. Here are two selections:

January, Brendan. *The National Mall.* (1972). Children's Press. Elementary.

Targ Brill, Marlene. *Building the Capital City*. (1996). Children's Press. Elementary.

"A History of US" is an eleven-book series of the history of America. It is a winner of the James A. Michener Prize in Writing. (1999). Oxford University Press.

Washington Online

A wealth of on-line information exists for travelers to Washington. Following are some most interesting for children:

http//www.loc.gov: The Library of Congress and check out the *Poetry 180* program initiated by Bill Collins, poet laureate. It is designed to help children read or hear a poem each day of the school year: *http/www.loc.gov/ poetry/180 http//www.aoc.gov/homepage.htm:* The United States Capitol site that provides information on the architecture and grounds surrounding the Capitol.

http//www.house.gov: The House of Representatives

http//www.senate.gov: The U.S. Senate

http/www.whitehouse.gov: The White House

http//www.si.edu: The Smithsonian Institution

http/www.washington.org: The Official Tourism site that gives you information on area events and places to visit.

http//www.washington-dc.travelpackets.com:

http//www.dcheritage.org: The D.C. Heritage Tourism Coalition provides lots of information on visiting D.C., including walking tours.

http//www.washingtonian.com: The site of the *Washingtonian* magazine provides information on where to go, where to eat and the comings and goings of Washington.

http//www.nps.gov: The National Park Service where you can find information on Rock Creek Park, Pierce Mill, the Old Stone House and more.

Chapter 6

WHERE ARE WE GOING NOW?

There are many ways to organize your family's visit to America's capitol city. One way our family enjoys bopping around the city is by neighborhood. By neighborhood? But I thought D.C. was all about government and federal buildings and, well, monuments, you may wonder. All true, yet Washington is made up of vibrant neighborhoods, each offering a distinct and tasty flavor of the city.

For example, Capitol Hill, or the Hill to the inside-the-Beltway crowd, is centered on the legislative branch of government – the Capitol Building, the House and Senate – and the judicial branch at the U.S. Supreme Court. But tucked away beyond the glimmer and glamour of national politics is the historic Eastern Market.

So Many Sights, So Little Time

From politics to parks, it sure is hard to see all you want to see in Washington, D.C. Here are a few recommendations for how to get the most out of a short trip to America's capital city.

Two-Day Itinerary

Day 1

Morning (4 hours): Begin early with a quick breakfast at your hotel. Then dash over to the **Capitol** by 8am to wait in line for time tickets to see the Capitol (Remember the Capitol does not open until 9am, but you must get there early to have a chance of getting in during tourist season). While one family member waits in line, the rest can jaunt down to explore the **Mall** or hike over to **Union Station** to pick up snacks at the Food Court. Another option is simply to send one family member out early to wait in line, while the rest join him or her later. Be the first to **tour the Capitol**. Have a quick snack. Then visit the **Library of Congress**, behind the Capitol, for a quick peek at some of the highlights.

Afternoon (3 - 4 hours): Eat lunch at the **Full Circle outdoor café** at the Hirshorn Museum. Enjoy the outdoor sculptures and huge, dancing fountain. Hike across the mall to the **Museum of Natural History**. Check on time tickets for the Insect Zoo or Discovery Room and any of the IMAX and Immersion Theater shows. Visit the dinosaurs, see the Hope diamond.

Evening: Have an early dinner at the outdoor **Pavilion Café** and take in the unique **National Gallery Sculpture Garden** (outdoors) and magnificent fountain. Hop a cab or take the metro to the White House. Since you can't tour the **White House**, it's best to go after the museums and other monuments close. It also is quite stunning to view in the early evening.

Day 2

Morning (4 hours): Send a scout (mom or dad) to wait in line to get free, time tickets to visit the Supreme Court, if the Court is in session. The rest of the family can enjoy a leisurely breakfast at your hotel. After visiting the **Supreme Court**, head down to the Mall to the **National Air and Space Museum**. Don't forget to see about IMAX tickets, unless you've bought them in advance.

Afternoon (4 hours): For lunch, either dine at the **Flight Line** cafeteria at Air and Space, or walk across the mall to the National Museum of American History and eat at the **Palm Court** – this is an old-fashioned ice cream parlor with spectacular ice cream treats for desert. Then, off on the monument hike. If you like a little exercise, walk to the **Washington Monument,** then straight across the street to the **Lincoln Memorial.** Nearby the Lincoln are the **Vietnam Memorial** on one side and the **Korean Memorial** on the other. Have a refreshing snack at the Reflecting Pool (there are rest room facilities).

Evening: Stop in at **Sequoia**, a restaurant at the waterfront in Georgetown, for a relaxing evening meal under the stars. Before or after dinner, stroll through **Georgetown** to enjoy the neighborhood or to shop, shop, shop!

Three-Day Itinerary

Use days one and two above, followed by:

Day 3

Morning (3-4 hours): This is **Tourmobile day**. Jump on and off at these stops – and more, if you desire: **Jefferson Memorial** (if you have time, rent the paddle boats), **Franklin D. Roosevelt Memorial, Frederick Douglass**

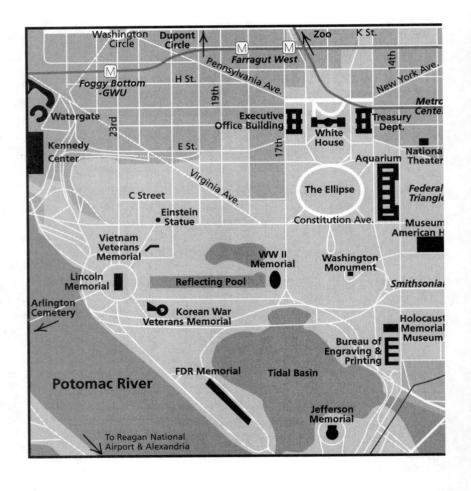

home, **Arlington Cemetery, Iwo Jima Memorial** and the new **World War II Memorial.**

Afternoon (3 hours): Lunch in **Dupont Circle.** Try **Teaism,** short-order and healthy, mainly Asian cooking, and lots and lots of tea. Walk two short blocks to the **Phillips Art Gallery** or **Textile Museum**. If there's time, stroll a few tree-lined blocks to the **Woodrow Wilson House,** for a bit of history.

Evening: Theater night! Your choice: **Shakespeare Theater, Kennedy Center, Warner Theater, Ford's Theater** (yes, where Lincoln was shot) and many more. If it's a Friday evening, the Kennedy Center has free performances at the **Millennium Stage.**

Five-Day Itinerary
Use days one through three above, followed by:

Day 4
Morning (2-3 hours): Let's go to the **National Zoo**. Get there as early as you can and peek in on the animals' early-morning regimen. The lions, tigers and gibbons are particularly active before 10am. The buildings open at 10am. Make sure you travel to Amazonia, the rainforest exhibit. Have a snack or early lunch at the Zoo.

Afternoon (2-4 hours) More adventure at **National Geographic's Explorers' Hall** – a short Metro ride from the Zoo. Then off to the **National Building Museum**, a favorite of our children, for something entirely different – another short Metro ride from Explorers' Hall. Have a snack at the Building Museum's café.

Evening: Travel up to the **National Cathedral** and stroll the grounds. Then, meander the few blocks over to dinner at fun and festive **Cactus Cantina.**

Day 5
Morning, Afternoon and Evening: Field Trip! Your choice. You can take AmTrack or drive to **Baltimore** to visit the aquarium, science center and other attractions. Or, travel to **Mt. Vernon,** George Washington's estate, and then visit **Old Town, Alexandria.**

So, off we go exploring the many treasures speckled throughout the neighborhoods of Washington, D.C.

CAPITOL HILL

THE CAPITOL
East from the Mall on Capitol Hill, 202/224-3121 (General number), 202/225-6827 (Capitol Tour Line, which gives up-to-date information on tours of the Capitol), www.thomas.gov. **Metro Stop**: Capitol South (blue line) or

Union Station (red line). Open for public tours from 9:00 am to 4:30 pm, Monday through Saturday. Time tickets are given on a first-come, first-serve basis at the kiosk located on the corner of First Street and Independence Avenue SW. The kiosk is open at 9:00am, one pass per person and the tickets are not given in advance. Enter on the side of the Capitol facing the Library of Congress, located on the opposite side of the Capitol Building that you would see if you are coming from the Mall. (Please note that at this time, numerous items including over-sized backpacks and duffel bags are not permitted on a tour of the Capitol and there is no place to check your items. Call 202/225-6827 to get current information on what is required to tour the Capitol.)

Politics and power lunches are a mainstay of life on Capitol Hill. Naturally, the Capitol Building and adjacent House and Senate office buildings are the hub of this neighborhood. But the Hill has a lot more to offer. Nestled around Capitol Hill, formerly known as Jenkins Hill, are the Library of Congress, the U.S. Supreme Court, the Botanic Gardens and Union Station, to name a few sites.

First things first. The boom of the gavel calls in this session of Congress.

The Capitol is the second-oldest building in Washington, D.C. (Can you guess the first?) In the late 1700s, Jenkins Hill was scouted out to be the perfect place to build the new nation's seat of government. But this was just the beginning of a long odyssey to complete the domed Capitol Building we all know today.

By 1800, the city of Washington became the permanent seat of government for this new nation and Jenkins Hill, the location to build the capitol's main buildings. Building a "federal Capitol" was the idea of Secretary of State Thomas Jefferson, who convinced President George Washington to construct the building. A design competition was called, with the design of Dr. William Thornton of the British West Indies, awarded first place.

Fun Fact: The word Capitol is derived from the highest of Rome's seven hills—the Capitoline. On this hill stood the Roman temple to Jupiter, completed in 509 B.C., the year the Romans gained control over the Etruscans, ushering in Rome's Republic era. The notion of a national "temple" devoted to public life is what Thomas Jefferson had in mind when he recommended the building of the Capitol to President George Washington. The Capitol should be "the first temple dedicated to the sovereignty of the people," Jefferson exclaimed.

Thornton's architectural design was neo-Roman, and his drawing of the Capitol was based on Rome's Pantheon. Construction began on September 18, 1793. Thirty-four years and $2,433,000 later found that the government had outgrown the original Capitol plan. The nation had grown from 13 to 31 states, and House and Senate chambers were much too cramped to properly conduct the business of the federal government.

A second design competition was held in 1850. America was rapidly growing and more room was needed in the building where our nation's representatives conducted business. Yet, no one proposal suited the grand plans of the Senate Committee on Public Buildings, so the top four ideas were merged into an overall plan. President Millard Fillmore proudly laid the cornerstone of the new extension on July 4, 1851. Senator Daniel Webster waxed eloquent on the launching of a new Capitol. He prayed that "the walls and arches and domes and towers, the columns and entablatures, now to be erected . . . endure forever."

In case you think political deal-making, swindling and petty politics is a modern phenomenon, think again. The building of the Capitol nearly collapsed due to political bickering over, well just about everything, including the political affiliation of the workers.

Somehow progress was made and in 1855, Thomas Ustick Walter, an architect who had submitted a design in the 1850 design competition, was given the go-ahead to create his cast-iron dome, now a worldwide symbol of American government. The dome was completed in 1863, capped off with a statue of Freedom (sculpted by Thomas Crawford), which continues to stand guard at the pinnacle of the dome.

With the Library of Congress moving from the Capitol to its own space in 1900 and the Supreme Court vacating its offices in the Capitol in 1935 to be relocated nearby, the legislative branch of our government finally had a grand home of its own.

Touring the Capitol

The guided tour is the "only deal in town" to see the inside of the Capitol, Tripp Jones from the Capitol's touring department told us. At the time of writing, self-guided visits are not allowed. The fun half-hour tour covers the Rotunda, Statuary Hall (the old House chamber) and the Crypt, which is the museum. We found the tour easy, accessible and short enough even for younger children. Those longing for more, can consider these resources:

Fun Fact: Traditions rule in Congress: Want to know how to tell which house of Congress is meeting? Look up. If an American flag is waving over the wing of the House (to the south of the Capitol) or the Senate (to the north), that house is in session. Here's another tradition. When the House is in session, a silver inkstand is laid on the Speaker of the House's table. It's the same stand that was first placed there in 1818.

Gallery Passes

One of the hottest tickets in town is a pass to the House or Senate Gallery to watch Congress at work. The Galleries are only open to the public when Congress is in session and you must obtain a pass from your Representative

or Senator. You can write or e-mail ahead of time (see Parent
we often have found passes available at the last minute by c
your Senator or Congressman the day before you want to vi'
foreign countries can obtain a pass at the office of the Sageant-at-A...
Senate or, on the House side, at the office of the Doorkeeper of the House.
Passports are required.

Fun Fact: Ever get in trouble for writing on your school desk? Well, if you
ever get a chance to examine some of the desks in the House or Senate Gallery
you may be surprised to find initials scratched into them from former members
of Congress who sat at them. We also hear that the desk where Jefferson Davis
once sat is bandaged on the side where a Union soldier slashed it with a
bayonet.

What is Congress?

Congress refers to the meeting of two separate governing bodies: the
Senate and the House of Representatives. Both chambers must pass legislation before it goes to the president, who can decide to veto or sign it into law.
Two senators are elected from each state. They are elected to a six-year term.
The number of representatives elected depends on the state's population.
California boasts 52 delegates, while tiny Delaware has only two. Representatives are elected for a two-year term. Because they are not states, the District
of Columbia and American territories, including Puerto Rico and Guam, are
represented by non-voting delegates.

Parent Tip

Find out more about your Congressman or Senator by visiting these
web sites: The official site for the U.S. Senate is www.senate.gov/html
From this site, you also can e-mail your Senators, check to see which bills
are being debated and learn more about the operations of the U.S.
Senate. The official House web site is www.house.gov/html.

THE SUPREME COURT

East Capitol and First Streets NE, 202/479-3298, www.supremecourtus.gov.
Metro Stop: Capitol South (blue and orange line) or Union Station (red line)
Open 9am to 4:30pm Monday through Friday. Closes weekends and federal
holidays. The Court hears oral arguments from 10am to noon and from 1pm
to 3pm from the first Monday in October to the last day of April. Opinions are
handed down through early June. On days the Court is only handing down
opinions, presentations begin at 11:30am. When the Court is not sitting, tours

are available from 9:30am to 3:30pm, run every hour on the half hour. For more information on tours call 202/479-3030.

Judge Judy fans trade legal insights with legal wannabes while waiting in line to see first-hand the comings and goings of the U.S. Supreme Court. This elegant, white-marble building, designed by Cass Gilbert, is in the style of a classic Greek temple – quite an impressive structure for children and adults. The two huge statues on either side of the 16 glistening, white-marble columns represent, on one side, *The Contemplation of Justice* and on the other side, *The Guardian, or Authority, of Law.* Look up. Inscribed above the columns is: "Equal Justice Under Law."

The Court consists of eight associate justices and one chief justice appointed by the President with the advice and consent of the Senate. Each justice is appointed for life. So far, America has had only 16 chief justices.

Parent Tip

Look in the *Washington Post* for the day's Supreme Court Calendar, typically found on page A3.

Fun Fact: Each justice gets to design his or her own chair. When a justice retires from the court, tradition calls on the other justices to chip in and purchase the retiring justice's chair as a parting gift.

Visitors enter the building through towering bronze doors, which boast sculpted panels illustrating historic scenes in the development of America's laws.

An introductory film, interesting but long for some children (24 minutes), runs non-stop at the ground-floor theater. The ground floor also is home to Supreme Court exhibits, which offer background on the history of the high court.

Time to Eat

A cafeteria is open from 7:30am to 10:30am and 11:30am to 2pm. A snack bar remains open from 10:30am to 3:00pm.

Time to Shop

A gift shop offers everything from backpacks with Supreme Court logo to ornaments resembling the huge bronze doors at the entrance of the Court.

Fun Fact: Prior to the completion of the Supreme Court Building in 1932, the court met in Philadelphia's City Hall, the basement of the U.S. Capitol, and a tavern!

Parent Tip

The Supreme Court's film is fascinating for many children. If, however, you are traveling with children of different ages and attention spans, one adult can occupy the non-film goers outside (one family we know engaged their little one counting steps, and columns and statues around the building) or at the cafeteria or snack bar. Bring one of their favorite paperback books to read. A gift shop, a good rainy day hideaway, is open from 9:00am to 4:25pm.

If you want to hear oral arguments before the justices, you have two lines to choose from. One line is for those wanting to stay for an entire argument (don't make this mistake, as we once did – you will never forgive yourself, and neither will your youngest of children whose whimpering and outright crying will be considered a high crime in this courtroom of all courtrooms!!). We recommend this option for young people seriously interested in the machinations of the high court. Be advised to show up at 8am for an oral argument that begins at 10am or 11am.

Another line is for a three-minute stop in the chamber. We highly recommend this experience for children who are able to sit still and be quiet for five minutes!! Even younger children are in awe of the spectacle of the nine judges seated in the red-velvet draped courtroom. An air of important decision-making in progress looms large in the Supreme Court's main theater – an impression will be made on your kids.

Public lectures in the main courtroom also are available when the court is not in session. For a precise schedule of public lectures, oral arguments and to see if the Supreme Court is open, call 202/479-3030 and choose 4.

Fun Fact: If you're lucky enough to get in to hear oral arguments, you may be surprised to hear a voice bellow: "Oyez, Oyez, Oyez." No, it's not a jazzy version of, "Oh, yes." It's the Supreme Court crier announcing that the Supreme Court is now in session.

LIBRARY OF CONGRESS

East Capitol and First Streets SE, 202/707-4604, or 202/707- 8000 for a recorded listing of special events. www.loc.gov. **Metro Stop:** Union Station (red line) or Capitol South (blue and orange). Open 10am-5pm Monday through Saturday. Closed Sundays and federal holidays. Visitor Center on ground level entrance in Thomas Jefferson Building at First St. SE between Independence Ave. and East Capitol Street.

Make the mistake we made. After living in D.C. for well over 10 years, we made our first (how embarrassing) trek to the Library of Congress just for this book. Little did we know that the Library of Congress was comprised of three, separate buildings – not even next to each other. We stumbled on the Madison Building (across Independence Avenue from the main Jefferson Building) thinking this was the main Library of Congress building. But, no. It only housed the Copyright Office. Oh well, we sighed, Nicholas Cage and his Hollywood entourage had closed the Jefferson Building for an afternoon soiree (!!) so we trooped up to the fourth-floor to (yawn, yawn) look at the copyright material.

Surprise! What fun!! There my children and their friends, Eliza and Suzanna, delighted in seeing the original Bert and Ernie finger puppets. Also on display are the original Pepsi Cola poster (1915), Monoply Game (Parker Brothers, 1954), Barbie and Ken (1961), *Creve Coeur – A Play in Two Acts* (Tennessee Williams, 1978), *Star Wars*, Episode Five script and posters (1979) – a big hit for my "I-want-to-be-a-filmmaker" 12-year-old son, to name a few. Another section included famous Supreme Court copyright cases, including King vs. Mr. Maestro, Inc., over Martin Luther King's "I Have A Dream" speech. (Our children were mesmerized by a copy of this landmark speech, with edits.)

Fun Fact: The Library of Congress has the smallest book ever printed, titled *Ant*. Guess how big the book is? You're right. The size of an ant!

Crossing the street to the ornate Jefferson Building is a treasure-trove of American and international literary and musical delights, which we toured days after Cage's Hollywood party. Children can see the first book printed in this country, the earliest surviving American photographic portrait, the first Disney comic book, the first baseball cards and the earliest motion pictures.

Perhaps the greatest treasures of the Library of Congress are the Gutenberg Bible and the Giant Bible of Mainz, displayed in separate cases in the East Corridor. Both were produced in Mainz, Germany, in the mid-1450s, one printed by hand, the other the first book printed with movable metal type. Other famous manuscripts are the numerous presidential papers, including one of Jefferson's drafts of the Declaration of Independence, Lincoln's drafts of the Gettysburg Address and Theodore Roosevelt's letters to his children.

Music is a highlight of any trip to the Library of Congress. Come see five Stradivarius violins and over 1,000 flutes. The American Folklife Center contains recordings of American music collected from "the hills and coves of Southern Appalachians, the Georgia Sea Islands, New Orleans jazz joints, cowboy campfires and religious gatherings.

Free concerts are offered usually twice a month. For a schedule call 202/707-5502. Tickets are $2 and can be obtained by calling 202/808-6900. Or, you can come to the Jefferson Building at 6:30 pm and wait in stand-by line on the evening of the performance.

Other highlights our children loved are: Houdini's magic diaries, note-books kept by Alexander Graham Bell, the National Digital Library Learning Center (America's Library site for children, www.americaslibrary.gov) and, believe it or not, Walt Whitman's notebooks. The Library of Congress has a Poetry Office and sponsors the nation's Poet Laureate. Louisa Gluck, a renowned teacher of poetry at Williams College, is the latest Poet Laureate. One of her latest books of poetry is *Vita Nova*, which was awarded the New Yorker Magazine's Book Award in Poetry. For more information on the Poet Laureate, visit http://www.loc.gov/poetry/laureate.html.

Parent Tip

Kids whining? Feet hurt, tummies empty, tears rolling. Take a time out together for a snack at the entrance to the Thomas Jefferson Building. You get a lovely view of the Capitol, they get some fresh air, food and a chance to be squirmy. Inside, children also enjoy the atrium, with its many trees and more-space-to-roam feeling.

Tours are available several times a day that allow you to see the grand Great Hall and the Main Reading Room. This is a spectacular building, with stunning staircases and stained glass ceiling, fabulous art work, marble columns and architecture at every turn. If your children need more flexible arrangements, use the self-guiding brochure or rent and audio tour. We found the later option more appealing to our youngest child.

A 12-minute film describing the Library of Congress can be viewed in the Visitors' Center of the Jefferson Building.

Time To Eat

A cafeteria and cappuccino bar are available only in the Madison Building.

FOLGER SHAKESPEARE LIBRARY

20 East Capitol Street SE, 202/544-4600 (public event info — dial 700, general information and directions – dial 5). www.folger.edu. **Metro Stop:** Union Station (red line) Capitol South (orange and blue lines). Open Monday through Friday from 8:45am to 4:45pm, Saturday from 10am to 4pm. Closed Sundays and federal holidays.

"What's past is prologue," surely holds true for the Folger. The library contains the world's largest collection of the works of William Shakespeare, as well as numerous rare books and manuscripts relating to the Renaissance.

Free docent-led tours last around 15 to 30 minutes. While the library is mainly for scholarly research, fun activities for little ones crop up every now and then. Remember, this is the Renaissance. Sword-fighting demonstrations have been scheduled. Caught anyone's interest?

A music series is presented from October through May, typically featuring Renaissance and Baroque compositions. A discounted ticket price is available for children and seniors. Call 202/544-7077 for box office information.

Parent Tip

Okay, you're into Shakespeare. Remember most of his sonnets from college. Known to use quotes from romantic tragedies as pick-up lines during your single days. But, alas, your children do not share your belief that Shakespeare is "such stuff that dreams are made on." Neither "rhyme nor reason" will convince them to tour the Folger. Visiting this library is their "winter of discontent." Sorry, have I done "too much of a good thing" with Bill the bard's words? The bottom line, you ask? Promise the little ones a long stop in the gift shop, if they let you revisit the days of the Renaissance and Shakespeare. Our children gave two decided thumbs up to the gift shop that dazzled them with Renaissance goodies, like swords and books and puzzles and games and unicorns!

For children interested in Shakespeare (and who can stay up past 10pm), the Shakespeare Theater is considered the nation's leading venue for reenacting the bard's plays.

UNITED STATES BOTANIC GARDENS

Maryland Avenue and 1st Street SW, 202/225-8333. www.aoc.gov. Open daily from 10am to 5pm. **Metro Stop:** Federal Center Southwest (orange and blue lines). This stop is three blocks from the Garden. The Garden is on the Capitol Grounds, between the Capitol Building and the Mall.

Take a break from politics and waltz into the refreshing, air-conditioned, and recently refurbished United States Botanic Garden. Often a relaxing relief from the squelching summer sun, the Garden has been a fun spot for our children since they were toddlers. So many flowers, so little time.

Bubbling fountains greet your entrance to the Gardens (bring lots of pennies). Indoor passageways lined with exotic flowers thrill kids of all ages. A special stop is the subtropical room (no air-conditioning here, be prepared for a hot, humid Amazon climate), with an amazing collection of orchids, their sweet perfume soothing your soul. Special exhibits also showcase medicinal, endangered, and primitive plants (Garden Primeval). As a youngster, my son delighted in the primitive plant collection, which were around during dinosaur days. At one point, he informed us of his desire to be a paleo-botanist!

Fun Fact: Chocolate? Where? Look for the chocolate tree. (Hint, hint: It's in the Garden Court.) Tiny white flowers grow on its branches, which develop into large pods from which to make chocolate.

The newly renovated building features a high-above-the-gardens walkway so you get a bird's-eye view of the exhibits. Lots of steps (the elevator sometimes is broken) to the "hey mom, this is like being at the canopy of a rainforest" view.

Call ahead or check the web site for special tours and lectures. Of special interest are the many family activities.

Fun Fact: The United States Botanic Garden is home to 4,000 living specimens!

Parent Tip
Food and drink are permitted only in the Garden Court and on the Terrace. This is a wonderfully, relaxing stop for a snack (bring your own, there's no food service). Close to Capitol Hill and the Smithsonian Museums on the Mall.

CAPITAL CHILDREN'S MUSEUM
800 Third Street NE, 202/675-4120, www.ccm.org. Metro Stop: Union Station (red line), about a 15- to 2-minute walk. If that seems overwhelming, take a cab from Union Station. Open Tuesdays through Sundays, 10:00am to 5:00pm. Closed on all Mondays during the school year, except the following Monday holidays: Martin Luther King Day, President's Day, Easter Monday, Columbus day, Veteran's Day and the Monday between Christmas and New Year's. Admission: $7.00 per person, $5.00 for seniors (55+), free to children under two years and members. Half-price on Sunday before noon with no other discount.

NOTE: By the time you have this book, the Children's Museum may be in the process of moving to a yet disclosed new location. Please call ahead to see if they are still operating.

Touch, feel, see, smell. The Capitol Children's Museum is hand-on education at its best. If your child has been hearing "don't touch" too often during your visit, here's the place to go where "please touch" is the rule.

Our kids love the permanent exhibits at the Children's Museum: the Mexican village complete with Mayan temple to climb and explore on the "shores" of a sandy beach. Children can be scientists at the American Chemistry *Chemical Science Center*, star in a cartoon in the Chuck Jones

Animation Studio, drive a Metro bus in Cityscapes, and go to a Japanese school in "Japan: *Through The Eyes of A Child.*"

Kids of all ages love climbing through mock sewers, sliding down a fire pole, be enclosed in a bubble (we did this, too!) and make paper flowers at the Mexico exhibit.

Before you go, check the web site for upcoming special events. They are "so cool," according to our children. A recent special event, for six- to 15-year-olds was to create a weather forecast in the museum's TV Studio. Children got to work with television equipment in front of the camera and behind the scenes.

Fun Fact: The Capitol Children's Museum's motto is a Chinese proverb: "I see and I forget. I hear and I remember. I do and I understand."

UNION STATION

Massachusetts and Delaware Avenues NE, 202/371-9441, www.us.net/dcnrhs/union.htm. **Metro Stop**: Union Station is a metro stop on the red line. Train station (Amtrak) is open 24 hours-a-day. Retail shops are open Monday through Saturday 10am to 9pm and Sunday noon to 6pm. Restaurants and other food-service shops have varying hours, but something is open even early in the morning and late at night. Parking garage (good place to park for Capitol Hill).

Our children love going to Union Station, even though they have lived in the D.C. area all their lives. It's a beautiful and grand station, bustling with the excitement of travel. Shops – clothes, crafts, jewelry, books, travel accessories, drug store and TOYS – abound. A food court, full of delights, is on the bottom level, but the station also boasts finer dining, all welcoming to children.

The station opened in 1907 with the arrival of a B&O Railroad passenger car from Pittsburgh, Pennsylvania (Barbara's hometown!!). It was modeled on Rome's Baths of Caracalla. The entire station was closed in 1981 because of its utter state of disrepair – a collapsed roof and an inside that began to look like the Botanic Gardens, with strange mushrooms growing through the floor. A magnificent renovation turned an eyesore into a splendid gateway to America's capital city.

Look for special events at Union Station. Every year around Christmas, we take our children to see the miniature train display, measuring a not-so-miniature 16- by 32-foot span. Four tiny trains travel non-stop through quaint villages, under snow-capped mountains.

Union Station also features nine movie theaters.

NATIONAL POSTAL MUSEUM

Corner of First Street and Massachusetts Avenue NE, 202/357-2700. www.si.edu/postal. **Metro Stop:** Union Station (red line, First Street exit). Open Monday through Friday, 10:00am to 5:30pm, closed Christmas day.

Stamp collectors – this is heaven. But the National Postal Museum is so much more – with exhibits that include holography, interactive computers and simulations of a Pony Express route. A permanent exhibit traces the more-interesting-than-expected history of mail delivery in the United States. Special exhibits have included the history of the Roberto Clemente stamp – he actually was honored twice, the first stamp issued in 1984 and the second in 2000. Check out the web site (click on calendar of events) for activities –many designed for children. Also, click on games for fun on-line games for kids – from postal history quizzes to decode the bar code games.

Fun Fact: The lovely poem you see carved into the building is called "The Letter," and it was written by former Harvard University President Dr. Charles Eliot (no it's not to the tune of the old song, *The Letter* – remember?– "give me a ticket for an airplane . . . my baby just wrote me a letter.")

Time to Eat
There is no food service in the museum, but just steps away is a plethora of restaurants and snack bars at Union Station. Or, for the wee-bit-of-the-Irish in you, cross the street to the Dubliner – a fine café.

Time to Shop
The gift shop is open seven days a week, from 10am to 5:30pm. Lots of postal souvenirs here. It's a stamp collector's paradise.

THE MALL

The Mall has it all: from a playful merry-go-round to NASA rockets, from 4th of July fireworks to fiery protests. This elegant and simple expanse of land running from the Capitol Building to the Lincoln Memorial is lined with precious elms and decorated with delicate cherry blossom trees.

The Mall welcomes visitors from around the nation and the world with its unfettered view; not a single skyscraper in sight. This open vista was the dream of Pierre L'Enfant, premier designer of America's capitol. A dreamer he was, for when he stood on Jenkins Hill (Capitol Hill) and looked out over the city, he only saw swamp and mud and bogs in a malaria-ridden field of nightmares. In his mind's eye, however, he envisioned the clean lines of the Mall that you gaze at today. It took tons of dirt to lift the Mall area from eight feet to about 22 feet elevation. The first permanent structure, the only one for some time, is the Smithsonian's red sandstone "Castle," completed in 1855, and now the cornerstone of the Mall.

During the Civil War, the Mall served as a staging ground for troops. Shabby wooden buildings were constructed, making the Mall an unpleasant extension of the city.

These temporary wooden structures were razed in the 1930s. Stately elm trees were planted and the first signs of L'Enfant's dreams of a "grand avenue" were beginning to take shape.

World War II saw the rise of more temporary buildings to house the growing war effort. Eventually, the Department of Interior's National Park Service was given the responsibility to oversee the construction and care of the National Mall, an increasingly difficult task as hundreds of thousands of people flock to the Mall for sundry reasons – protestors to tourists.

The earliest protestors to descend on the mall were the women's suffrage movement and the Bonus marchers, jobless World War I veterans who demanded payment of veterans' bonuses. Martin Luther King's world-renowned "I Have A Dream Speech," which attracted over 250,000 people, was delivered from the Lincoln Monument.

As a public forum, the Mall also hosts numerous festivals, which feature dancers, artists, crafts people and chiefs from around the world.

The Mall is also home to the 1940 Allan Herschell-model merry-go-round. We have been riding this charming carousel since our children were babies and they – and us – never tire of it. A wonderful treat after a long stay indoors at one of the Smithsonian Museums, located on either side of the Mall.

SMITHSONIAN INSTITUTION

Tenth Street and Jefferson Drive, 202/357-2700 (real person!) Dial-a-Museum 202/357-2020 (English), 202/633-9126 (Spanish), www.si.edu, **Metro Stop:** Smithsonian (blue orange line, mall exit) or, for Air and Space and Hirshorn the closest Metro stop is L'Enfant Plaza (blue, orange, yellow, green lines, Maryland Avenue and 7th Street exit), Museums open daily from 10am to 5:30pm. Closed Christmas Day. Summer hours may be extended. Information desk at Castle opens at 9am.

"Mommy, this is more fun than an amusement park," squeaked my little girl as she went through the Brain exhibit, one of many special, amazingly hands-on exhibits, for her third time. Children love the Smithsonian museums.

Parent Tip
The Mall must have been set up with parents in mind. Just when your children are on the verge of collapse from too much touring, you can step outside onto the wide open fields of the Mall and run, jump, play frisbee, and just get all the wiggles out before re-entering for round two of sightseeing. Snack vendors are everywhere. Or, bring your own and picnic outside. My son's favorite snacking place since he was a toddler is the swan bench located between the Ripley and the Arts and Industry Building. Can you find it?

☞

There's something for everyone: dinosaurs, spaceships, American history, art, butterfly garden, surprising outdoor sculpture, ice skating (more on that later!) and the great outdoors just steps away.

So, here we go on a tour of the Smithsonian:

The Castle

Ask a cab driver to take you to the Smithsonian and he inevitably will drop you off at what locals call the Castle. No surprise. It looks just like a castle! The Castle, completed in 1855, is the original Smithsonian Institution Building. It was designed by James Renwick Jr., an architect who also designed St. Partrick's Cathedral in New York City.

The Castle is made of red sandstone from Seneca Creek, Maryland, in the 12th-century Norman style (a combination of late Romanesque and early Gothic). For many years, this single building housed all aspects of the Smithsonian, including an exhibit hall from 1858 until the 1960s. It also served as home for the first Secretary of the Smithsonian Joseph Henry and his family.

The Castle was nearly destroyed in 1865, when a fire raged through the structure. Renovation included fireproofing in 1884. In 1901, the city's first children's room was opened in the Castle's South Tower Room. You still can see the original decorated ceiling and stencils. Today the Castle houses administrative offices, the Commons (which used to be a dining room) and the Smithsonian Information Center.

The Commons is no longer open as a dining room, which is a sad development. Right now, Smithsonian officials are debating how to use this charming room. It resembles a chapel with its high vaulted ceiling and curved apse, yet it was never used for this purpose. Upon its completion, it was used as a library. Around the walls of the Commons, are coat-of-arms of famous people. They include William Penn, William Shakespeare, Sir Francis Drake, Edmund Burke, Sir Issac Newton and Charles Darwin, to name a few. Visit the information center for a pamphlet to help you match coat-of-arms with famous personality. By the time you visit the Castle, maybe you will be able to get a glimpse of this lovely room.

The **Castle's information desk** is a great first-stop before embarking on what could be a marathon day at the Smithsonian. Want to know where to find the Hope diamond? They can tell you. Need directions to the metro, bathroom, museum, special exhibits, food services? They know all. Information material is available in numerous languages, including Spanish, French, Arabic and Chinese. We have found the folks who staff this information center some of the kindest, most helpful people in all of our travels!! Three cheers!

Fun Fact: Jim Smithson, an English chemist and mineralogist who died in 1829 and left in his will a provision "to found, at Washington, under the name of the Smithsonian Institution, an Establishment. . .", never visited America, let along the Smithsonian Institution. In 1904, Alexander Graham Bell traveled to Genoa, Italy, where Smithson was buried and brought his sarcophagus to the United States, where it now resides in a chamber off the north foyer of the Castle. Do you know what mineral was named after Smithson (Clue: it's a zinc ore)? Check your answer with the good people at the Castle's Information Center.

Remember that each museum has its own schedule of activities. Check the information desk at each museum, even if you have stopped at the Castle's information desk.

Parent Tip

Ask the Information Desk staff for the "Exploring African American Heritage" brochure. This pamphlet highlights the African American experience in the arts and sciences by noting special exhibits and activities.

ARTS AND INDUSTRIES BUILDING

900 Jefferson Drive. Tourmobile Stop.

You won't miss this building, and hopefully it will be completely renovated by the time you visit (currently, it is closed for renovation.) Directly outside is the carousal, beckoning to you and your children with its magical pipe-organ tunes. Inside, you may remember, used to be another child-friendly activity: **Discovery Theater**. The Theater recently moved to a location right behind the Castle, through the garden on the right side of the building. The standard is high, the shows both entertaining and educational. To order tickets and get schedule information call 202/357-3030. Information also is available at www.discoverytheater.org.

The Arts and Industries Building over the years has been the dress rehearsal hall for exhibits that eventually have been relocated to other museums. For awhile, spacecraft was housed here, then moved to the newly opened Air and Space Museum. Later, the first exhibits of the African American Museum project were located here, only to be moved when the African Museum opened. Currently, Arts and Industries houses many special exhibits—a recent one on the brain was unbelievable and lots of fun for children.

FREER GALLERY OF ART

12th Street and Jefferson Drive. www.si.edu/collections/freer.htm.

In 1923, the Freer Gallery of Art opened and became the first art museum of the Smithsonian. It was founded as a gift to the nation from

Charles Lang Freer. The collection focuses on American and Asian art. Currently, it is closed.

SACKLER GALLERY
1050 Independence Avenue. www.si.edu/activity/planvis/museums/aboutsga.htm.

The Sackler Gallery opened its doors in 1987 as a result of the benevolence of Arthur M. Sackler MD, a New York medical publisher. Dr. Sackler gave the Smithsonian innumerable Asian treasures, including bronzes and jades from China, some dating back 4,000 years; paintings from the 10th to the 20th century; pre-Islamic metalware from the ancient Near East; and several stunning sculptures from South and Southeast Asia.

Check out the web site for concerts, lectures and children's activities.

Just for Kids: ImaginAsia is a splendid way for children to spend several weekend hours. These programs are typically offered on Saturday or Sunday for children age 6 to 14. One example of a weekend children's program is called the "Year of the Horse." Children, accompanied by a parent or other adult, explore the Freer and Sackler collections of horse, lions and dragons that are part of festivals. Next they gather at the museum's classroom to create stick puppets of lions or dragons to take home. We have found these activities as interesting as the kids! It also gives one parent the chance to explore on his or her own.

HIRSHORN MUSEUM AND SCULPTURE GARDEN
Independence Avenue and 8th Street SW. 202/357-2700 (from 10:00am-4:00pm). 202/357-1618 (after-hours tape). www.hirshorn.si.edu. Sculpture Garden open from 7:30am to dusk.

Wildly modern art stretches your imagination as you tour this museum. Kids go blah if you mention an art museum? Try the Hirshorn. Its art and exhibits are different, exciting and accessible. How can you miss with Calder's child-like sculptures, or George Segal's "Bus Riders." How about Andy Warhol's "Marilyn Monroe's Lips? Say, "Happy Birthday, Mr. President."

Find Tony Cragg's "New Figuration." Cragg loved to collect plastic pieces. For "New Figuration," he simply stuck plastic pieces directly on the wall, forming a rich, kaleidoscope of colors. (Hmm, think the little ones might try this at home?)

The Hirshorn was made for fun. It's design – like a doughnut – allows artwork to be exhibited inside and out. Look high above the fountain and see the tightrope man. And, the fountain. Huge, watery, mesmerizing, tempts kids – and you on a typical Washington summer day – to jump in.

The Hirshorn is ringed with intriguing sculptures. Particularly fun are Juan Munoz's "Conversation Piece," rolling human figures engaged in – I don't know what, but clearly enjoying life outdoors.

Across the way and down below is the Sculpture Garden. We took our children their since they were babies. My son, especially, was taken by the bigger-than-life sculptures. From Joan Miro to Rodin, all made for a fun frolic around the Sculpture Garden. Now, my children enjoy the sculptures by drawing them, or re-naming them, or simply skipping around the paths (no running, please).

Perhaps the best family packet I have ever seen is available at the information desk of the Hirshorn. The "Family Guide was created by Diane Kidd and Maryanne Del Gigante and serves as a self-guided tour that helps parents introduce modern art to young children in a most interesting way. The packet includes 14 art cards that introduce a work of art, shows its location and presents activities to enhance a child's understanding and appreciation of the art. Hats off to you, Diane and Maryanne!

Check at the information desk, on-line or by phone for special children's activities, including animation features for youngsters.

Time to Eat

A great place to snack during summer months is the **Full Circle** outdoor café. Shaded from the sun, with a spectacularly huge fountain in view, the café offers welcome relief for ansy boys and girls.

Parent Tip

Check the web, information desk, or phone 202/357-3235 (ext.114) for details on the museum's Young at Art workshops for children age 6-9 with adult companion.

NATIONAL AIR AND SPACE MUSEUM

7th and Independence Avenue SW. 202/357-1400 (Office of Tours and Reservations) 202/357-1686 (Theater and Planetarium) www.nasm.si.edu **Metro Stop:** L'Enfant Plaze (red line) or Smithsonian (blue, orange line) Open 10:00am to 5:30pm. Daily, except December 25.

"A small step for man" turns into a full-day excursion for your family! This is one of the most popular museums on the mall – so expect crowds and lines. The Smithsonian Institution's National Air and Space Museum (NASM) maintains the largest collection of historic air and spacecraft in the world. As soon as you walk in, you will be dazzled by the Apollo 11 command module (how did they fit in there?), Lucky Lindy's (Charles Lindberg) "Spirit of St.

Louis," the original Wright 1903 Flyer and other air and space wonders dangling overhead. You can even touch a 4-billion-year-old Lunar rock sample.

It would be easy to marvel at each and every aeronautic wonder at Air and Space for days. Here are a few suggestions and highlights to help economize your time. First, check at the information desk. Ask for the detailed *Museum Guide* and select the appropriate choices. Enjoy knowing more about the beginnings of air travel? Then check out Pioneers of Flight (room 208), where you can see an exhibit on Lindbergh or Amelia Earhart's Lockheed 5B Vega, among other displays. Want to know more about planes and war? Go see Sea-Air Operations (room 203), Legend, Memory and the Great War in the Air (room 206). Space travel your thing? Then, visit Rocetery and Space Flight (room 113) or Space Race (room 114) or Apollo to the Moon (room 210). "Feel the need for speed?" You may want to stop in at Beyond the Limits (room 213). Got your eyes on the stars. See Explore the Universe (room 111), Exploring the Planets (room 207). These are just some of the rooms available.

Audio tours are available in English, French, Spanish, German and Japanese. Our younger children always are too busy looking at all the air and space exhibits to listen to the tours. However, they do help parents provide children with interesting tid-bits here and there. The Audio Tour kiosk is located near the Information Desk at the Independence Avenue entrance to the Museum. Standard rate per headset is $5.00; $4.50 for students w/ID, senior citizens, NASS and Smithsonian Associates members.

Our children rated the following as the best at Air and Space:

How Things Fly: Better than an amusement park, you will be hard pressed to get your children out of this exhibit. It's hands-on education fun at its best.

Lockheed Martin IMAX Theater: This is "television" any parent will let their children watch. BIG screen (seven stories wide and five stories high), coupled with fantastic footage makes for a pleasant voyage. Films include To Fly and Cosmic Voyage are mainstays. Other special films also are featured. Current as of this writing, *Adrenaline Rush: The Science of Risk* and *Helicopters in Action: Straight Up* are playing at this IMAX. Regular admission rates are: $7.50 for adults, $6.00 for youth/senior. There is a group discount for a

Parent Tip

Tickets for the IMAX and Einstein Planetarium can be purchased up to 2 weeks in advance. Do this if you can. The ticket lines are so long, you and your children will feel as if you could have gone to the moon and back before tickets are in hand. (call 202/357-1686 or 202/357-2700 for info and ticket purchase). This is especially frustrating if you only have a little time at the museum.

family of four or more: $10.00 youth/senior. A Theater/Planetarium (see next entry in this book): $12.00 adult, $9.00 youth/senior. $5.50 per ticket. Other specials include: IMAX double feature: $13.00/adult.

Einstein Planetarium: The closest thing to space travel. The Einstein Planetarium is equipped with the unique Zeiss VI planetarium projector, with complex optics that re-create the stars, the five planets closest to Earth and other celestial objects that can be seen in the night sky by the naked eye. Sound and visual effects add to the starry spectacle. Opened in April 2002 is the Planetarium's newest show, Infinity Express, narrated by Laurence Fishburne, that has you skim the planet Mars and blast through the intergalactic void. Tickets are $4.00/person, no discounts.

Docent Tour: We were quite surprised that our then seven- and ten-year-old so enjoyed the docent tour. Fun facts abound and, although they were the only children on the short tour, the docent warmly welcomed them and answered their special questions when the tour was over. Maybe we had a great guide, but it's worth a try. You can always leave if the kids get bored. Free docent-led tours are given daily (10:15 and 1:00) and depart from the Tour Desk, South Lobby. For more information on all tours, call 202/357-1400.

Fun Fact: Missed the Star Wars: Magic of Myth exhibit that toured in 1999? It was soooo popular, we took a group of our son's friends through the exhibit (twice) for his birthday. Well, excerpts of the audio tour narrated by none-other than James Earl Jones (of course he is the voice of Darth Vadar, despite all those phone commercials) are available on-line at www.nasm.si.edu Click on "former exhibitions."

Time to Eat

The Flight Line cafeteria is fun, festive with food on the go! The cafeteria is encased in glass, letting in lovely views of the Mall and Capitol. While the kids were not so hot on the pizza, they rated high the fries and —surprise, surprise — the salad.

Time to Shop

A BIG, BIG hit with kids of all ages is the gift shop at Air and Space. Budget enough time to look around at the great planes, rocket ships, kites, games, books, puzzles, space food (we say yuk, the kids liked it!) and much more. The newly renovated shop consists of three levels of goodies. You can even see the original Starship Enterprise model from the Star Trek show.

STEVEN F. UDVAR-HAZY CENTER

14390 Air and Space Museum Parkway, Chantilly, Virginia (at Dulles Airport), open 10am to 5:30pm, every day except December 25. Admission:

Free, public parking is $12. A shuttle bus service runs between t and Museum and the new Center for a fee. www.nasm.si.ed
Want to wow your kids – including teens? Take the time to ' F. Udvar-Hazy Center (what a name – but he's the guy who w~~~~ ~~~ ~~~~~ for this museum!) The Center has it all – over 80 aircraft and dozens of space artifacts, including the "Enterprise" space shuttle and the World War II "Enola Gay" that changed the face of war. Don't forget to visit the Wall of Honor, a permanent memorial with the names of thousands of people who contributed to America's aviation and space exploration.

But, wait, here's the clincher for all you Top Gun addicts. Swagger up to one of the flight simulators if you "feel the need for speed" and experience how it feels in the cockpit of one of several aircraft. Tickets for this thrill ride run about $7.00 per person for each four-minute ride. Another fun ride is the SpaceWalk 2004 3D orbital journey around the 16 nation International Space Station. Price of a ticket is about $6.00 These simulators are not for the faint of heart, or people with back and neck pain or who are pregnant. You also must be 42 inches tall to ride, unless accompanied by an adult. The lines are long, as you can imagine, for these joy rides, especially on the weekends.

For those of you who do not crave living dangerously, spend some time at the Donald D. Engen Tower, an observation tower with a 360-degree bird's eye view of Dulles International Airport. What a view – of planes taking off and landing. An elevator transports about 15 people at a time every five minutes. Strollers are not permitted on the elevator – there is a stroller parking lot near the elevator. Again, expect loooong lines. No tickets required.

Check the Welcome Center for information on tours, led by docents or do-it-yourself on tape. A food court should be open when you visit. Currently, Subway sandwich shop services the Center.

NATIONAL MUSEUM OF NATURAL HISTORY AND THE NATIONAL MUSEUM OF MAN

10th Street and Constitution Avenue NW. 202/357-2700. www.mnh.si.edu, **Metro Stop:** Smithsonian (blue, orange line, walk across the mall to the museum), Archives/Navy Memorial (green and yellow line), Open 10am to 5:30pm daily, except December 25.

During our son's nascent dinosaur stage, we practically took up residence in this museum. We knew every bone, let alone every dino. Save this museum as a special surprise for all your young paleontologists. Yet, there is so much more.

Enter on Madison Drive, rather than Constitution Avenue, to be greeted by an enormous African bush elephant. He stands 13-feet tall and when he was alive (yes he is real) he weighed 12 tons. We can never look at this spectacular specimen again without chuckling over our son, who at the age of 3 in the loudest voice a little one can muster, tugged on his mommy's sleeve

̴nd exclaimed, "Mommy, look at that elephant's BIG, . . ." We'll let you fill in the blank. So, be prepared for anatomical observations.

Of course, many of your children will pull you onward and forward through dino land. Ask at the information desk, if real, live paleontologists will be working the day of your visit in Dinosaur Hall. They can be seen in a glass-enclosed office on the left-hand side. Here are some other highlights of the museum:

O. Orkin Insect Zoo: It's a room full of insects. From cockroaches (ugh) to tarantulas (double ugh), the kids and most parents have a blast in this room. Our family is particularly mesmerized with the bees, whose hive you can see through a glass window. There is a tube that leads to the outdoors and all the worker bees travel back and forth bringing home their wares to their Queen. Can you find her? Volunteers conduct tarantula feedings and let visitors touch and hold some amazing insects. We found this as amazing as the kids! For more information, you can e-mail the Insect Zoo staff at insectzoo@nmnh.si.edu Also, check at the information desk as soon as you enter to see if free timed tickets are needed for the Insect Zoo.

Discovery Room: A wonderful hands-on experience for younger children who delight in the wonders of the natural world, the Discovery Room recently underwent renovation. Explore different cultures, open up "discovery boxes" to see and touch items from the natural world. Peer into the jaws of a crocodile (no longer alive, of course). Your kids, like ours, will think they've gone to heaven.

African Voices: This is a brand-new interactive hall on African history and cultures.

Mummies: Peek, if you dare, at the display of animal mummies. Can you find the one our children say looks just like Jabba the Hut? Several short films describe the mummification ritual and practice for those future Indiana Jones'.

Janet Annenberg Hooker Hall of Geology, Gems and Minerals: Remember, the Museum of Natural History also is home to the Hope diamond (whoa, this is one large diamond) and other rocks and minerals. Our children have taken school trips to this exhibit and have enjoyed the many rocks, minerals and other geological specimens. The section recently was renovated to include interactive computers, animated graphics, touch-me specimens and film presentations. Check out the Whole Earth Theater's production.

Johnson IMAX Theater: Great films on this IMAX screen. Current selections include Africa: The Serengeti, Cirque de Soleil's The Journey of Man, Galapagas in 3D and, for all you parents, the Rolling Stones. Ticket prices typically are $8.00 for adults, $7.00 for youths (2-17) and seniors (55+). However, special features, such as the Rolling Stones, are $11.00 for everyone. For more information, call 202/633-2700 or e-mail imax.johnson@nmnh.si.edu

Immersion Theater: Totally awesome technology. This is a new large-screen interactive educational game. You become a player in the game and get to make responses to navigate your character through the film. Unbeliev-able fun. Better than any gameboy. Ticket prices: adult: $5.00, youth (2-17) and seniors (55+) $4.50. For more information, call 202/633-7400.

IMAX and Jazz Night: Our family has spent several fun Friday evenings at the museum, enjoying a film and settling down for dinner and jazz at the Atrium Café. The food is a cut above typical museum cafeteria fare and is served in a "mommy-they-have-linen-tablecloths" atmosphere. Jazz Night runs from 5:30pm to 10:00pm, with the last IMAX show beginning at 9:00pm.

Time to Eat

Besides the lovely Atrium Café, the museum runs a more typical large-scale cafeteria, never a favorite of our little ones. If you can, run next door to the Museum of American History to eat in their old-fashioned Ice Cream Parlor or outside at the Pavilion Café, next to the large fountain and one of the outdoor sculpture gardens.

Time to Shop

Dinosaurs, lots and lots of dinosaurs. Big, scary ones. Soft and cuddly ones. Need I say more. Besides a fantastic children's section, the gift shop has many special finds for adults. Check out the educational videos and books.

NATIONAL MUSEUM OF AMERICAN HISTORY

14th Street and Constitution Avenue NW. 202/357-2700. www.americanhistory.si.edu. **Metro Stop:** Smithsonian (blue and orange lines) or Federal Triangle (blue and orange lines). Open daily 10:00am to 5:30pm, closed December 25.

From the original Star-Spangled Banner to Archie Bunker, this museum is about American history, politics and culture. Our children quickly head for one of the two interactive centers upon each visit to the museum (more later). They also are especially attracted to the science halls on the first floor. How fast does light travel? Find out at On Time. What distress message did wireless operators aboard the Titanic send? Check your answer at the Information Age, wireless

Parent Tip

To get the most out of this museum, remember that your youngest children will not feel as strong a connection with Archie Bunker's chair or Martin Sheen's (*West Wing*) jacket. So do steer them to Dorothy's ruby slippers and the Hands on History Room and Hands on Science Center.

☞

telegraph department. Another area focuses on chemist Marie Curie and her discovery and pioneering use of radium in medicine.

The American Presidency is a fascinating collection of memorabilia from the desk on which Thomas Jefferson drafted the Declaration of Independence to Chelsea Clinton's ballet slippers. The entire exhibit is filled with interactive experiences, some of which captivated our youngest child.

Hands on History Center

Second floor. Open from noon to 3:00pm, Tuesday through Sunday, closed federal holidays. Tickets are required on weekends and other busy days. Pick up the free, timed tickets at the door to the Center.

Learning is experiential in this room filled with more than 30 activities that help children explore the daily life of the American past. Our children particularly enjoy taking White's Efficiency Test to see if they are quick enough to be a postal clerk on the railroad in 1870 (This is Little House on the Prarie time, for all you Laura Ingalls fans!). They also get a kick out of climbing up on a high-wheel bicycle and pedaling to send a telegraph message.

Hands on Science Center

First floor, west wing. 12:30pm to 5:00pm Tuesday through Friday and 10:00 to 5:00 Saturday and Sunday, closed Monday.

Science rules in this center. Separate DNA from a cellular solution. Investigate carbon dioxide through dry ice and your breath. Explore the use of lasers in compact disk players. Families can roam on their own, or participate in small-group experiments with knowledgeable staff. Lines can be long. We've found that getting here at the end of the day actually is less crowded than any other time.

Time to Eat

Well, there is a cafeteria (lower level). But, our children always beg to go to the Palm Court, a charming, old-fashioned ice cream parlor (first floor). The etched glass, with scenes of swans and egrets, is lovely. Hot dogs, mac and cheese, pizza are children love. Ahh, then comes the ice cream. A Star-Spangled Banana Split, Inventor Sundae, Clown Sundae. Yum, yum.

Time to Shop

History buffs and science lovers will particularly enjoy this gift shop. So do little girls who devour Little House or American Girl books or other historical fiction.

NATIONAL MUSEUM OF AFRICAN ART

Independence Avenue SW (across from the Sackler). 202/357-4600. www.si.nmafa.edu **Metro Stop:** Smithsonian (blue or orange line) Open daily 10:00am to 5:30pm, closed December 25. Tours: Tours are offered on a walk-in basis Thursdays at 5:00pm (summer only) and Saturday and Sunday at 11:00am and 1:00pm. Call 202/357-4600, ext. 222 for more information.

Step into a fascinating adventure in Africa. Masks, drawings, wood sculpture, a stunning permanent collection of cast metal, wood, bronze and ceramic tantalize even the youngest travelers. Besides the wonder of each exhibit, our family has always enjoyed the emphasis on children at this museum. Call the information center (202/357-4600) for a schedule of children's activities, including art projects and storytelling.

Also, ask at the information desk for a copy of the museum's Family Guide, a great way to begin an exploration of African culture and people.

Time to Eat

There are no cafes at the African Art Museum. Food services are available at the nearby Castle, Air and Space Museum or across the Mall at the Natural History and American History Museums. Or, simply buy some food from the many vendors and have a picnic in the garden outside the museum.

Time to Shop

Two thumbs up from our children on the gift shop. A great selection of books and toys, colorful crafts, posters, jewelry and records and tapes.

Art Night on the Mall

An experiment with extending summer hours every Thursday evening has turned into a huge success at the Smithsonian. From Memorial Day through Labor Day, the following museums are open until 8:00pm: Freer, Sackler, African Art and the Hirshhorn, on Thursday evenings. Musical performances, children's activities, films and gallery talks are featured, with much taking place outdoors. It's a great time to enjoy early evening festivities with your children, and gaze at a lovely sunset over the Washington Monument. For a schedule of activities, call 202/357-2700 or visit www.si.edu/activity/artnight.

ENID A. HAUPT GARDEN

Tenth and Indepenence. 202/357-1926. **Metro Stop:** Smithsonian (blue and orange lines, either Mall exit or Independence Avenue) Open daily 7:00am to 8:00pm during the summer, 7:00am to 5:45pm in winter months. Garden tours are available Sunday at 2:00pm, weather permitting.

A peaceful escape from a hectic day of touring. If you can take the summer heat, these gardens are a wonderful place for snack time. We always snack on the charming black-iron swan bench located behind the Castle. On unbearably hot days, let your little ones slowly gallop through the tiny fountain that squirts from the ground, outside the side door of the Arts and Industry Building. Nearby, let your children discover the animal-shaped topiaries, including huge bison. Then stroll around to the front and inhale the sweetness of the Smithsonian's rose garden.

THE NATIONAL GALLERY OF ART

6th Street and Constitution Avenue NW. 202/737-4215. www.nga.gov, **Metro Stop:** Judiciary Square (red line), Archives (yellow or green lines) and Smithsonian (blue and orange). or Archives (red line), Open Monday through Saturday from10am to 5pm and Sunday from 11am to 6pm, Closed December 25 and January 1, **Entrances:** The East and West Buildings are connected by an underground concourse with a moving walkway. Entrances to the West Building are on the Mall, on Constitution Avenue at 6th Street and on 4th Street. The entrance to the East Building is on 4th Street. There are 6 public entrances to the Sculpture Garden: one entrance on Constitution Avenue at 9th Street, N.W.; three entrances on 7th Street, N.W.; one directly across from the Gallery's West Building entrance; and two entrances on the National Mall between 7th and 9th Streets, N.W. **Tours** by Special Appointment may be arranged for adult groups of twenty or more by calling 202/842-6247.

Concerts take place at 7pm Sunday. Concert-goers are admitted to the West Building, East Garden Court, at 6pm, first-come, first-seated. The entrance at Sixth Street and Constitution Avenue remains open until 7pm and the Garden Café is open until 6:30pm. For recorded information, call 202/842-6941.

How embarrassing. Not until we began to write this book did we realize that the National Gallery is not part of the Smithsonian Institution! Throughout the 1920s and early 1930s, Andrew W. Mellon collected art with the intent to create a national gallery of art located in Washington, D.C. He commissioned architect John Russell Pope in 1935 to draft sketches of a new national gallery. At his death in 1937, Congress, through a joint resolution, accepted Mellon's gift and the National Gallery was born. President Franklin D. Roosevelt opened the West Building of the new National Gallery of Art on March 17, 1941.

In 1978, the Gallery's East Building was open to accommodate the growing collection. It also houses administrative offices, a library and a research center. Keeping it all in the family, the building was financed by Mellon's children, Paul Mellon and the late Ailsa Mellon Bruce.

This building was designed by I.M. Pei and stands in stark contrast to the West Building's classical look. The East Building represents modernity. Both, however, share pink marble from the same Tennessee quarry.

Fun Fact: During the 1940s, the Gallery's most famous paintings and sculptures were evacuated to the Biltmore Hotel in North Carolina for wartime protection.

Private donations continue to keep the Gallery growing. In 1999, the Morris and Gwendolyn Cafritz Foundation contributed the innovative outdoor Sculpture Garden to be enjoyed all year round. Don't get confused over sculpture gardens – there are two. One is across from the Hirshorn, next to the carousal (look under the Hirshorn for information on their sculpture garden).

The **National Gallery's Sculpture Garden** is, not surprising, next to the National Gallery. It is fanciful and fun. The pieces are out-of-this-world large. Find the huge spider (Louise Bourgeois). Reflect at the *Great Rock of Inner Seeking* (Isamu Noguchi). Marvel at Lichtenstein's house of illusion. You'll love the humor in Barry Flannagan's *Thinker on a Rock*, a witty interpretation of Rodin's *Thinker*, although your little ones will conjure up images of Alice in Wonderland. "What is that?," your children will shout. And, you'll give away your age by knowing that the giant red circle with shags of black hair is a – typewriter eraser!! – this one by Claes Oldenburg and Coosje van Bruggen.

Fun Fact: In 1967, the Gallery received one of its most famous paintings: Leonardo Da Vinci's *Ginevra de/Benci* through the Ailsa Mellon Bruce Fund.

Our son's favorite: George Rickey's *Cluster of Four Cubes*. Its simple geometric design that magically sways with the slightest breeze captivates children who always want to know how things work. The Sculpture Garden is open Monday through Thursday from 10am to 11pm Friday and Saturday from 10am to midnight and Sunday, 11am to 9pm.

Information guides with descriptions and locations of each sculpture are available at the main 7th Street entrance of the Sculpture Garden and at all art information desks.

Parent Tip

If you visit D.C. between November 15 and March 15, take your children to the National Gallery of Art Sculpture Garden ice-skating rink. In warmer months, the rink is a huge fountain. Enjoy a hot chocolate after at The Pavilion Café or do what a good friend, Milena and her two children, Jan and Misha, do after an afternoon of skating– visit nearby Chinatown for a good Chinese dinner. Hours are Monday through Thursday 10am to 11pm, Friday and Saturday 100am to midnight and Sunday 11am to 9pm. Admission is $5.50 for adults and $4.50 for children, students with ID and seniors 50 and over. Skate rental is $2.50.

Parent Tip

How lucky you are. If your children decide to melt down just as you are finding inner calm inside the National Gallery, designate one parent to take the kids outside. Sounds like the "outside" parent got the shorter straw? Not at all. You can take them to the outside **Sculpture Garden**. What fun you'll have following the little path to discover the wonders of this garden. Don't forget, there also is the Pavilion Café for snack time.

Like the Smithsonian, the National Gallery is an incredibly child friendly museum. Our children are fortunate to have one of their friend's mothers, a former curator, organize art trips during the school year when the schools are out. Through Milena's generosity and clear understanding of how to make art accessible to children, our little group of kids (who started out as mainly third-grade squirmy, wiggly, soccer-playing boys and now are middle schoolers, still a bit wiggly, but so engaged in the world of art!) have come over the years to enjoy touring art museums with little more than a sketch pad and colored pencils. For those family's not lucky enough to have Milena take your children to the museum, the National Gallery has done the next best thing – create remarkable art adventures that keep your child busy, helps them learn something about art and gives you time to enjoy one of the loveliest art museums in the world.

Immediately upon arrival, stop at the information desk and ask for the **Postcard Tour** for your children. At the East Building you will receive the "Things that Walk, Talk and Squawk" and at the West Building information desk you will get the "American Art Search" packet. The goal is to hunt for the art that is on the postcard. In our "Italy with Kids" book we recommend that you stop in the gift shop first, purchase postcards of art in the museum, and take your children on a treasure hunt. At the National Gallery, the postcards are already put together for you. Just remember to return the packet before you leave.

Another option for your family is to rent the **Adventures in Art Audio Tour**, designed with children in mind. Your children will travel with Pieter and Tanya as they "explore life and art nearly four hundred years ago in Holland and today's Belgium." The audio can be rented at the Acoustiguide desk located in the West Building Mall Entrance. $3.00 per tour. You can rent additional headphones for $2.00, although it better be an I-love-my-sibling day before you plug two or more of your children into one tape. Our adventures with Pieter and Tanya turned into the War of the Worlds before we wised up and rented a separate tape for each of our little darlings.

Info & Micro Library is a service we never thought would be child friendly. Our children proved us wrong. This is a service that clearly is a boon for true art lovers. Located on the main floor of the West Building, the Micro Library is an easy-to-operate interactive computer system that allows visitors to search for their favorite artist, artwork or major theme by a mere touch of the finger. You get lots of info on the artist and artwork, plus a map that shows where the art you are interested in is located. You can also design a personal tour of the museum, with a printout of location. Our little girl just loves cats. So she searched for cats and found oh-so-many matches. We spent a cat-lovers day seeking the frisky felines hiding in paintings and sculpture all over the National Gallery.

You can also purchase for $2.50, the paperback **Family Guide: West Building Highlights**. The National Gallery staff has chosen a few favorite works of art to share with you. These works introduce your family to different artists, styles, and subjects — some tell stories, some describe people, places, or things, some are about color and design. As you explore the galleries with this guide, you can decide which works of art you like best and why. Activities include looking at the art of El Greco, Sir Peter Paul Rubens, and Joseph Mallord William Turner. We enjoyed this publication as much as the children. (It was made possible by a grant from the Vira I. Heinz Endowment.)

Parent Tip

Free, high-quality family workshops led by local artists or museum staff, are offered over many weekends. Most activities are for children in the 6 to 12 age range. All require an accompanying adult. Call 202/789-3030 or visit the National Gallery's web site at www.nga.gov for a schedule and registration information.

Another Sunday program is called Stories in Art. This activity for children age 4 and up combines storytelling with looking at art and a hands-on activity. Offered at 11:30 and repeated at 1:00, each program lasts approximately 45 minutes. For more information, call 202/842-6880. No registration necessary. However, it fills up quickly, so come at least 15minutes early.

Fun Fact: The National Gallery of Art has a cool kids' web site, called NGAkids. The web site has something for children of all ages, including older students who may need art research for a class assignment. Check it out.

Time to Eat

There are lots of selections at the National Gallery of Art. Perhaps the best indoor option for children is the **Cascade Café**, serving soups, salads, wood-fired pizzas, specialty sandwiches, hamburgers, hot dogs, and fresh-baked desserts. A full espresso bar features homemade gelato, panini, and sweets. This cafeteria-style seating comes with a unique view, a cascading waterfall that falls in from the outside. Your little ones will be mesmerized by the falling water. Don't worry: The water cascades behind a glass screen.

Hours: Monday through Saturday, 10am-3pm and Sunday 11am to 4pm. Espresso and Gelato Bar: Monday through Saturday 10am to 4:30pm and Sunday 11am to 5:30pm.

Our favorite spot since we were young and single is the serene **Garden Café.** Seating is around a lovely water sculpture encircled by beautifully arranged flowers and plants. While this is not the place for highly active, let's –play-hopscotch-while-we-eat-children, it is a lovely spot to go with sleeping babies or children who are able to relax with you for a peaceful lunch. Hours are Monday-Saturday 11:30am to 3pm, Sunday noon to 6:30pm. They may be finished with their renovation by the time you visit.

Do remember, however, that if even your quietest children have spent an entire day touring sites with little time to hop and jump, it may be better to eat at the Cascade Café or, better yet, outside at the Pavilion Café.

The **Pavilion Café** has outdoor seating, wonderful views of the sculpture garden and glorious fountain, which freezes into an ice rink in the winter. Inside, it is light and airy, with floor-to-ceiling windows. Food is above standard for typical museum cuisine, although there is pizza, sandwiches, salads, cookies and ice cream. Beer and wine also are available. Hours are Monday through Saturday 10am to 5pm and Sunday, 11am to 6pm . During the skating season, the café is open until 9pm Monday through Saturday and until 7pm on Sunday.

Stay for the jazz on Fridays (5pm to 8pm). It's a great way to unwind after a long day of being a tourist. The lamp lights encircle the fountain, creating a romantic atmosphere for you and a whimsical evening for your children.

Time to Shop

The National Gallery of Art offers several gift shops. The Children's Shop, on the concourse level of the West Building, particularly has a large selection of books, games, puzzles and unique art kits. The other gift shops in the West Building are located on the ground floor and the concourse level. The East Building gift shop offers items related to special exhibits.

The teacher in Barbara could not pass up the *National Gallery of Art Activity Book*, with 25 adventures in art. Filled with puzzles, games, quizzes and so many opportunities for children to make their own art, while learning about many of the great masterpieces. You can purchase the book ($16.95) at any of the gift shops.

THE NATIONAL ARCHIVES

700 Pennsylvania Avenue NW, 202/501-5000, www.nara.gov. **Metro Stop:** Archives (yellow and orange), Closed for renovation.

The National Archives, located across the street from the National Gallery of Art's Sculpture Garden, is a visit you will always remember. On view, and tightly guarded, are America's founding documents: The Declaration of Independence, the Constitution and the Bill of Rights, recently restored. Two stunning murals by Barry Faulkner depicting the presentation of the Declaration of Independence and the Constitution have been restored, as well.. The display cases for the Charters of Freedom – the Declaration of Independence, the Constitution and the Bill of Rights – also were reconfigured, allowing all four pages of the Constitution to be displayed (previously only the first and last pages can be displayed), and making the Declaration of Independence, the U.S. Constitution and the Bill of Rights accessible to visitors with disabilities.

Lines can be long, and security is tighter than ever, but it is a remarkable experience especially for school-aged children who are studying the birth of a nation. Our visit certainly left an imprint on the hearts and minds of our grade-school kids.

Oh yes, if you want to do research on your family tree, this is the place to go. Just remember, children under 16 are not permitted in the Research Room.

BUREAU OF ENGRAVING AND PRINTING

Fourteenth and C Streets SW, 202/874-3019, www.bep.treas.gov or www.moneyfactory.com. **Metro Stop**: Smithsonian (blue line), All tours must be arranged up to one week in advance by calling 202/874-2330 or 1-866-874-2330.

Show them the money! This is one of the most popular tours in D.C. In a long line you will snake through corridors peering through windows where people are . . . making money. Lots of it! (We even got to watch people eating lunch!) The tour's structure – walking through and reading signposts about the printing process – is best suited for older children. Particularly annoying is a tape that is played overhead giving pertinent information about the process, but is pretty much blocked out by the ohhs and ahhs of kids and adults remarking on the stacks and stacks of bills.

Fun Fact: Did you know that the last time a $10,000 note was printed was in 1947?

The end of the tours halts at the door to the gift shop. Need a humorous gift for tightwad Uncle Ralph? Stop here for a bag or bottle of shredded bills. Stamp collectors should check out the postage stamps available for purchase.

UNITED STATES HOLOCAUST MEMORIAL MUSEUM

100 Raoul Wallenberg Place, 202/488-0400, www.ushmm.org. **Metro Stop: Smithsonian** Open daily from 10am to 5:20pm., Tours: Time passes are required only to enter the permanent exhibit. You can visit special exhibits, including the children's section without a pass. For passes, either get them the day of your visit, or call ahead to order: 800/400-9373 or visit www.ushmm.org and clicking on visit, then tickets.com

Heart-wrenching exhibits. Expect to be moved to tears. This is for families who want to teach their children about this tragic part of world history.

Congress authorized the building of the United States Holocaust Museum in 1980 to be a permanent, living memorial to all who perished in the Holocaust. The museum houses permanent and temporary exhibits, two theaters, an interactive learning center, research facility and memorial space and classrooms.

Children 8 and up are encouraged to visit Remember the Children: Daniel's Story, which **you do not need a timed pass to see.** Remember the story helps children understand the Holocaust through a narrative journey with Daniel.

Do take your children to see the Children's Tile Wall, also known as the Wall of Remembrance. Over 3,000 tiles painted by American children inspire you to remember the children and to discover ways to bring about peace and tolerance. The Wall, dedicated in 1993, is located in the lower level.

Other exhibitions for children are the multi-media Wexner Learning Center and the 14-minute introductory film.

The architecture of the Holocaust Museum is innovative and metaphorical. Architect James Ingo Freed designed the museum after visiting numerous Holocaust sites. Architectural allusions to the Holocaust are subtle and made to "take you in its grip," says Freed.

The permanent exhibition, The Holocaust, presents a comprehensive history of the Holocaust through photos, artifacts, film, oral history and filmed eyewitness testimony. It is recommended for children age 11 and up.

Family Sundays is a program for children age 9-12 who, with their parents, want to learn more about the history of the Holocaust. Reservations are required: Call 800/400-9373. Admission is free, but there might be a service charge.

Note: The museum is most crowded from April through the end of July. The best time to come is late afternoon during the week.

Time to Eat

The Museum Café in the Ross Administration Building, adjacent to the museum should re-open by the time you have this guide. It will have been fully renovated. You also can purchase snacks at any of the food vendors parked on 14th Street. No food or drinks are allowed in the museum.

Time to Shop

The gift shop has a good selection of books and m(children, that feature the history of the Holocaust and of tradition.

THE MONUMENTS

Many of America's national monuments are located on or around the Mall, making for a relatively easy walking tour. However, summer days can get extremely steamy and often little ones do not enjoy long hikes. Tourmobile to the rescue. Each and every monument is reachable by the Tourmobile, a National Park Service narrated sightseeing bus service that stops at all major points on the mall, Capitol Hill, Arlington Cemetery and so much more. Even as denizens of America's capitol city, we enjoy the light and lively quips and tales of the Tourmobile drivers and the fact that we don't have to go desperately seeking a parking space at each site. There are other companies running tourmobiles, but we still enjoy the original. So here we go, off to see the city's major monuments.

WASHINGTON MONUMENT

15th Street at Madison, 202/426-6841, www.nps.gov/wamo/, **Metro Stop:** Smithsonian (blue and orange lines), Open Memorial Day to Labor Day from 8am to 11:45pm and the rest of the year from 9am to 4:45pm, Closed December 25, **Tickets:** You must get tickets to enter the Washington Monument at the kiosk on 15th Street and Madison. These are free. Or, order to tickets in advance for $2 per ticket by calling 1-800/967-2283, or visiting www.reservations.nps.gov, Please note you cannot bring strollers, suitcases, backpacks larger than 18x16x8, or food/drink of any kind, including un-opened bottled water. For health concerns, please see a Park Ranger.

Barbara remembers her eighth-grade field trip to Washington, D.C. A highlight was racing up the steps of the monument – the only girl joining a flock of boys. That's 896 steps!! While, we don't recommend this absolutely inappropriate behavior (!) for your children, the Washington Monument remains a sight to behold.

Today's visitor to the monument dedicated to the Father of America, will not be able to jaunt up the steps. The stairs were closed during the 1970s. All visitors are ushered into an elevator that will take them up to a magnificent view of America's capital city.

Fun Fact: The Washington Monument is a 555-foot tall marble obelisk. Visitors take an elevator to the 500-foot level for a panoramic view of the city.

ʒome visitors decline the ride, and instead admire the monument from ʋutside. The white-marble juts up from a point on a tiny hill that sits between the Capitol and the Lincoln Memorial. Surrounding the monument are 50 American flags, one for each state, dutifully blowing in the breeze. A lovely time to come is when the cherry blossoms are in bloom, many of the delicate trees surround the base of the hill where the monument is perched. Also, look for the New York City Fire Fighters Memorial Stone.

The monument was designed by architect Robert Mills, who in 1836 won a competition. His initial design was much more elaborate, with "a grand circular colonnaded building 100 feet high, from which springs an obelisk shaft... making a total elevation of 600 feet." The shaft was based on Egyptian obelisks, with a single star near the apex to represent Washington's immortality. The final form is much more simple and elegant. Elaborate ceremonies marked the laying of the first stone on July 4, 1848, and sparkling fireworks have followed ever since. The Washington Monument is the place to be for Fourth of July celebrations.

Ask a Park Service Ranger for a Junior Ranger booklet. These booklets will help families visit the Mall and several of the monuments.

LINCOLN MEMORIAL

West end of Mall, between Constitution and Independence Avenues, 202/426-6895, www.nps.gov/ncro. **Metro Stop:** Smithsonian (blue and orange lines, Mall exit), Open 24 hours a day, with a Park Ranger on duty from 8am to midnight and 9am to 5pm from Labor Day to Memorial Day. Closed December 25.

Climb the steps to the Lincoln Memorial, turn around and gaze out at the reflecting pool, the Washington Monument and beyond to the Capitol. It's a take-your-breath-away view. Imagine the area packed with over 250,000 people and you see what Martin Luther King gazed upon when he delivered his poignant I Have A Dream speech.

As lovely as the view is by day, it is stunning at dusk, with the white marble of the Washington Monument standing stark against the deepening sky streaked with ribbons of pink and orange.

You also will feel the enormity of the structure once you walk inside. The columns in the colonnade stand at a height of 44 feet. The dazzling white marble structure resembles a Greek temple. In 1912, the Lincoln Memorial Commission, created by Congress, decided on Henry Bacon to be the architect and in 1914, the Commission called on Daniel Chester French to be the sculptor. Bacon, an admirer of Greek architecture, turned the classic Greek temple to its side, thus creating an entryway to the Mall.

Initially, French's plans called for sculpting a Lincoln figure about 10 feet tall. After a review of Bacon's large-scale plans, French realized his figure of Lincoln would be dwarfed by the structure. French quickly doubled the size of his sculpture. He and Bacon also discussed how to present Lincoln –seated or standing. They agreed that Lincoln should be seated, with a look of struggle on his face that would reflect the burdens of a civil war. Since no single piece of marble was found for such a colossal sculpture, 28 block of white Georgia marble were joined together so precisely that no seam appears visible.

Fun Facts: Which famous speeches are inscribed on the inside walls of the Lincoln Memorial? The Gettysburg Address and Lincoln's Second Inaugural speech.
There are 36 columns surrounding the monument, representing the 36 states of the Union when Lincoln was president.
Did you count 56 steps leading up the monument? That's how old Lincoln was when he was assassinated.

A most remarkable picture of the Lincoln Memorial is re-printed in the Lincoln Memorial official handbook of the National Park (page 41, $4.50, found in the memorial's museum shop). It shows the Lincoln Memorial surrounded by swamp, a far cry from the stunning setting created to pay tribute to America's 16th President.

RELFECTING POOL AND CONSTITUTION GARDENS
Between the Washington Monument and the Lincoln Memorial. www.nps.gov.
This is one of our family's favorite spots. We used to bike past the Reflecting Pool to work from our apartment in Adams Morgan to jobs on Capitol Hill. Our children learned to ride their bikes on this path and the meandering walkways through Constitution Garden. We dubbed our strolls through this garden "Duck and Goose Walk" because of the many ducks and geese who also enjoy the calm of this urban garden. It is a peaceful, tranquil, tree-lined oasis in the center of a fast-paced, buzzing city. A grand place for a picnic or merely to rest weary feet.
Make sure you find the six-acre lake, just a winding footpath away from the Reflecting Pool. The island in the center of the lake is a memorial to the signers of the Declaration of Independence and it is a refuge for many of our geese and duck friends.

Parent Tip
During the summer months, a vendor sells food for the ducks and geese. Please refrain from giving them human food, which is more difficult for them to digest. Constitution Gardens also has a kiosk that sells food for humans and a well-maintained rest room (thank goodness!!).

VIETNAM MEMORIAL

Constitution Gardens, 202/619-7222, **Metro:** Smithsonian, mall exit, Open daily.

Controversy swirled around the design of a memorial to Vietnam veterans. Was it too little, too much? Over the years, the black-granite, V-shaped memorial has come to honor loved ones lost in Vietnam with dignity through its simple design. Inscribed on the dark, yet shiny, granite walls are the 58,156 names of those who lost their lives during the war. Mothers, fathers, sisters, brothers, wives and now, grown children of those who died, gather at the Memorial to pay homage. Anytime of year you can find flowers, notes, pictures left by loved ones who have not forgotten after all these years. These special gifts are collected and displayed in the Museum of American History (third floor). It is a touching site, and children (and adults) are asked not to run through the paths or ride their bikes here.

The memorial was designed in 1981 by Maya Ying Lin, an architecture student at Yale University. One arm of the V points to the Lincoln Memorial, while the other toward the Washington Monument. A sculpture of three young soldiers, sculpted by Frederick Hart, guards the entry to the memorial. Books are located at each end of the V that can help you locate the panel where each name is inscribed. The names are listed by the year each died in alphabetical order.

KOREAN WAR VETERANS MEMORIAL

Between the Washington Monument and the Lincoln Memorial, on the opposite of the Reflecting Pool from the Vietnam Veterans Memorial, 202/426-6700 or 202/619-7222, Open daily.

Nineteen ground troops striding toward victory comprise this war memorial. A 164-foot mural wall is inscribed with the caption: "Freedom is not Free" and is etched with photographic images of nurses, chaplains, crew chefs and others who provide support for a war effort. The memorial is situated in a 2.2-acre site, adjacent to the Lincoln Memorial.

WORLD WAR II MEMORIAL

Located at the Rainbow Pool at the east end of the Reflecting Pool between the Lincoln Memorial and the Washington Monument, 1-800/639-4WW2, www.wwiimemorial.com. Open Daily.

They are known as the "greatest generation" — the men and women who came of age during our nation's fiercest international battle for freedom since the Revolutionary War. Finally, there is a memorial that heralds their collective courage, discipline and self-sacrifice. The World War II Memorial opened on 29 April 2004 and was formally dedicated one month later on 29 May. Over 300,000 people gathered for the dedication.

Architect Friedrich St. Florian was the winner of a design competition for the memorial. Bronze and granite dominate the structure. Kershaw stone was selected for the vertical elements. The stone is quarried in South Carolina. For the main plaza paving stone, Green County was selected and it is quarried in Georgia. Accent paving on the plaza is done in two green stones – Rio Verde and Moss Green, both quarried in Brazil.

Sculptures around the memorial include four bronze eagles, 24 bronze bas relief sculptures along the ceremonial entrance and 4,000 sculpted gold stars on the Freedom Wall.

It is a stunning tribute to the 400,000 who died in the war and the millions who supported the war effort from the homefront. A great book to read that captures the essence of World War II and the impact the war had on individual lives, as well as the nation and the world at large, is Tom Brokow's The Greatest Generation.

THOMAS JEFFERSON MEMORIAL AND TIDAL BASIN

East Potomac Park, 14th Street and East Basin Drive SW, 202/426-6822 or 202/426-6841, www.library.thinkquest.org, **Metro:** Foggy Bottom (blue line), Open daily, April through September from 8am to 11:45pm and October through March from 9am to 4:45pm, closed December 25.

The classical design of this domed monument is based on Mr. Jefferson's own architectural drawings, which resemble the President's home in Monticello, Virginia. It overlooks the Tidal Basin, where paddle boats churn away during summer and spring. Come at cherry blossom time and you're in for a visual delight. Dainty, pink and white cherry blossoms decorate the walkways around the Tidal Basin. Cherry blossom time is around late March or early April. A festival is held to celebrate the 1,233 Yoshing cherry trees given by the people of Japan.

Fun Fact: In 1999, denizens of Washington were perplexed over a politically jarring incident. Someone was chomping at the cherry blossom trees. The crime scene showed clear marks around the base of the trees. "I cannot tell a lie," said the criminal. Well, maybe not. Turns out a family of beavers – mom, dad and baby –were the culprits. The National Park Service gently re-located the furry fiends to another patch of federal waters with more appropriate cuisine.

Architect John Russell Pope conceived of the Jefferson Memorial, basing his drawings on the Pantheon and Jefferson's design for his Monticello home. Three marbles were used: the outside consists of Vermont Imperial Danby marble, the interior uses Georgia White marble and the floors are done in Tennessee Pink marble.

The dome provides a haven for a 19-foot bronze statue of Jefferson, sculpted by Robert Evans. Evans decided to present Jefferson in a standing position to represent his looking out into the world. Besides being a President and framer of the country, Jefferson was an architect, farmer, educator and writer – a true Renaissance man.

Look up at the entrance of the memorial at the bas-relief sculpture. It represents the Declaration Committee – Thomas Jefferson, John Adams, Benjamin Franklin, Roger Sherman and Robert Livingston. These men were appointed by Congress to draft the nation's Declaration of Independence. Jefferson took the lead on this task in part due to his excellent writing skills.

Fun Fact: Next to the monumental Jefferson Memorial is the modest and obscure memorial to George Mason, the only Founding Father not to sign the Declaration of Independence. See if you can find out why?

Jefferson's writings are etched into the interior walls, including the first quote from the Declaration of Independence: "We hold these truths to be self-evident. . . " Other quotes are from letters to colleagues ("God who gave us life gave us liberty." letter to George Washington and "I am not an advocate of frequent changes in laws and constitutions, but. . . letter to Samuel Kerchevel). The last quote inscribed on the walls ("Almighty God has created the mind free.") is taken from a 1771 Bill for Establishing Religious Freedom.

Fun Fact: President John F. Kennedy once remarked to a gathering of Nobel Laureates that they were the greatest assemblage of talent in the White House, except when Jefferson dined there alone!

Parent Tip

Do rent the paddle boats. Once our son and Barbara ventured out on a cool, summer day (a rarity) to read part of Treasure Island. Anthony loved paddling all the way to the end to sneak his boat into the hanging branches, pretending to be searching for treasure. What fun! You can rent paddle boats from the end of March through the end of October, from 10am to 7pm, daily. (202/479-2426).

FRANKLIN D. ROOSEVELT MEMORIAL

Cherry Tree Walk, across the Tidal Basin from the Jefferson Memorial, 202/376-6704, www.librarythinkquest.org **Metro:** Foggy Bottom stop (blue line), Open 24 hours daily, staffed 8am to 12pm.

Unique among monuments, the FDR Memorial is totally outdoors and shaped into four rooms, each representing one of FDR's presidential terms.

Cascading waterfalls, small reflecting pools and black granite are integrated to make this an enchanting and striking legacy for FDR. It is, not ironically, the first memorial planned to be entirely wheelchair accessible.

Fun Fact: Believe it or not, this is the first memorial to honor a first lady, Eleanor.

In 1955, Congress passed a resolution stating their desire for a memorial to FDR. The memorial opened its doors 42 years later in 1997.

The first outdoor room, represents FDR's first term and his New Deal for the American people as a vehicle to ride out of the Great Depression. In the second room is a haunting representation of the bread lines and the agony felt by those humiliated by the need to wait in the lines for a meager rationing of food. FDR's fireside chats also are depicted in this room.

The third room finds FDR in a wheelchair, partly covered by his cape. Roosevelt in a wheelchair stirred quite a controversy during the development of the monument. Remember FDR contracted polio in 1921. The room is filled with wartime FDR quotes, since this was the beginning of World War II. The fourth and final room depicts the end of World War II and the death of FDR. The enchanting waterfall flowing into a series of pools blends eloquently with FDR's quote: "More than an end to war, we want an end to the beginnings of all war." This room also pays tribute to Eleanor Roosevelt.

HAINS POINT

East Potomac Park, Across the street from the Jefferson Memorial.

Just another place to view the cherry blossoms? Actually, Hains Point is so much more. There is a golf course, tennis and a playground. But the main reason to come here is to see the fantastic sculpture called *The Awakening*. It is a half-buried GIANT man, with arms reaching upward as if to claw his way out from the sinking earth. Beyond the giant are the moody waters of the Potomac. This is photo-op heaven. Children love to climb over his limbs. Barbara's first site of the giant sculpture, created by Seward Johnson, was in the middle of one of the first 10K Run for the Cure events. Needless to say, the shock of *The Awakening* surely shaved minutes off her time (nice try, huh?)

DOWNTOWN I: WHITE HOUSE & ENVIRONS

From the White House to the Department of Interior Museum, from the Treasury Building to the Corcoran Gallery of Art, downtown D.C. is more than lawyers and lobbyists. The streets are on a grid – letters run north-south and numbers, east-west. Only the state-named streets may cause confusion because they run on angles, dissecting the other streets at different intervals along their route. So, off we go first to what will surely be your premier place to visit.

THE WHITE HOUSE

1600 Pennsylvania Avenue, 202/456-7041, www.whitehouse.gov. **Metro Stop:** McPherson Square (blue line), Tours available for groups of ten or more.

West Wing fans – here's your chance to see the real thing, well sort of. Better than the Hollywood set, the White House is an impressive structure.

Security demands now allow group tours of 10 or more through one's member of Congress. They are self-guided tours and can be accepted up to six months in advance. If your group is scheduled for a self-guided tour, stop at the White House Visitor Center first, lcoated at the southeast corner of 15th and E Streets, open from 7:30 to 4:00. Call 202/456-2121 for updates on tours, since the rules may change at any time.

While you gaze on the outside structure, here are a few details to contemplate. The White House is the oldest public structure in the District of Columbia –its cornerstone was laid in October 1792. It is made of Virginia sandstone painted white. James Hoban, the architect, designed the president's mansion in the style of an Irish Georgian country house.

Since that first brick was laid, remodeling has been the name of the game at the White House. President Jefferson added the terraces. Andrew Jackson built pipes for running water. Franklin Pierce – central heating. Rutherford B. Hayes added, can you believe it, the first bathroom and first telephone.

Fun Fact: Thomas Jefferson, using a pseudonym, submitted plans for a design of the White House. He lost the bid.

However, the most dramatic changes came after the British burned the White House in 1814 during the War of 1812. Rebuilding of the burnt structure was completed in 1817, with Hoban leading the task. In 1902, the architectural firm of McKim, Mead and White oversaw the redecoration and reconditioning of the State Rooms. At this time, the presidential offices were removed from the East Wing and the West Wing was established. The West Wing includes the Oval Office, the Cabinet Room, the James S. Brady Press Briefing Room and executive offices for the president's staff.

During Harry Truman's tenure, the presidential family actually moved across the street to the Blair House for major renovation to take place. The interior was gutted, new foundations laid and a steel framework was erected.

Fun Fact: On November 1, 1800, President John Adams became the first president to live in the White House. He and his family froze due to the unfinished walls. Thomas Jefferson, the next president to reside in the White House, quickly fit fireplaces with coal-burning fixtures.

ELLIPSE

Behind the White House, **Metro Stop:** Mcpherson square (blue line). The Ellipse is the site of the National Christmas Tree and Christmas tree display from each of the states. It is a grassy field – a fun spot for running about after lots of hours touring the city.

OLD EXECUTIVE OFFICE BUILDING

17th Street and Pennsylvania Avenue, 202/395-5895, **Metro Stop:** Farragut West (blue line).

Our children call it the wedding cake house. It actually is a flamboyants French Second Empire building, and one of the older government buildings in the city. Constructed from 1882-1888, it originally housed the War, Navy and State Departments. Today it holds offices for the White House staff.

Fun Fact: The Old Executive Office Building is the building where Oliver North shredded key documents during the Iran-Contra scandal.

DEPARTMENT OF TREASURY

500 Pennsylvania Avenue NW, 202/622-089, www.ustreas.gov/curator,. **Metro Stop:** McPherson Square (blue and orange lines) and Metro Center (blue, orange and red lines). **Tours:** Suspended. Visit the web site, click on curator and then virtual tour for an on-line tour of the building.

Washington Monument architect Robert Mills also designed this Greek Revival structure, made of granite. The building is the current office for the Treasury Department, but also contains the 1864 Burglar-Proof Vault and the Cash Room, a two-story marble banking room.

Fun Fact: The temporary office used by President Andrew Johnson following Abraham Lincoln's assassination has been restored to its 1860 appearance and is located in the Treasury Building.

DEPARTMENT OF INTERIOR MUSEUM

Eighteenth and C Streets. 202/208-4743. www.doi.gov. **Metro Stop:** Farragut West (blue line)

Home on the range, and so much more, defines the Department of Interior. DOI (ahh, the alphabet soup of Washington, D.C.) oversees America's natural resources. The Department of Interior is steward of public lands, parks and wildlife programs. It also is home to the Bureau of Indian Affairs.

A tour of the museum is special because it is customized to meet the needs of your party –be they from 2 to 20. Museum staff recommend that a tour that includes children in 2nd grade and younger go no longer than 45 minutes. For those able to handle more detail, the tours can run up to a little over an hour.

You must call ahead to make an appointment. Tours take place between 8:30am and 4:30pm from Monday through Friday and the third Saturday of each month from 1pm to 4pm. Adults (16 and older) must bring photo ID.

Highlights of the museum include dioramas showing historical trailmarks, including westward expansion and Native American life and culture. Our children particularly enjoyed seeing Native American kachina dolls and headdresses.

DAUGHTERS OF THE AMERICAN REVOLUTION MUSEUM

1776 D Street, 202/879-3241, www.dar.org, **Metro Stop:** Farragut North (red line, 17th Street exit). Open 8:30am to 4pm Monday through Friday. Saturday hours are planned. **Tours:** Weekdays from 10am to 2:30pm. Call to check for Saturday tours.

The Daughters of the American Revolution Museum (DAR) is the city's only American decorative arts museum. Open in 1890, the 33 rooms depict early American life. The museum showcases items made or used in America prior to 1840.

Our children especially enjoyed the costumes and toys. Anyone reading American Girl or Little House stories or other historical fiction will love to see what life was like in days gone by. The New Hampshire Attic is of most interest to children. Displayed in the room are furnishings, toys, games and dolls that span over 150 years of childhood delights.

Parent Tip

Visit the playroom, where children of the 21st century can play with toys from the 1700s. This is a favorite stop for youngsters!

AMERICAN RED CROSS VISITORS CENTER

1730 E Street NW, 202/639-3300, www.redcross.org, **Metro Stop:** Farragut West (blue and orange lines) and Farragut North (red line), Open Monday through Friday from 9am to 4pm, **Tours:** Tuesdays and Fridays 9am, for one-half hour. Free.

This is Clara Barton territory. While Barton did not originate the Red Cross idea, she was the first person to establish a Red Cross Society in America in 1881. Barton pushed the organization beyond its initial mission of providing battleground assistance to including disaster relief. She served as the Red Cross's first volunteer president until 1904.

Barton and others lobbied President James Garfield to sign the Geneva Convention, and although he agreed, he died before the signing took place. The Geneva Convention, eventually adopted in 1882, gave the American Red

Cross an official base of inclusion in the International Red Cross and the Red Crescent Movement. The United States was the 32nd nation to sign the agreement, which agreed to protect wounded soldiers during wartime.

The museum includes thousands of artistic and historic objects that chronicle the past and present roles of the American Red cross in nursing, international services, armed forces emergency services, biomedical services and disaster services.

Time to Shop

Visit the gift shop for more information on Clara Barton (good book project topics!) Also, check out the cool, historic posters of the American Red Cross.

RENWICK GALLERY

Pennsylvania Avenue at 17th Street NW, 202/357-2531, www.americanart.si.edu. **Metro Stop**: Farragut West (blue and orange lines), Farragut North (red line), Open daily 10am to 5:30pm. Closed December 25, **Tours:** Call three weeks ahead to schedule tours.

This charming art gallery features American art and craft. Part of the Smithsonian Institute, it actually predates the Smithsonian museums. It's extensive collection of American art – think Georgia O'Keefe, Jacob Lawrence, Edward Hopper, Mary Cassatt, to name a few – clearly reflects the ethnic, cultural and geographic diversity of America.

Fun Fact: The building used to be the Old Patent Office Building where inventors, like Thomas Edison, sought patents for their marvelous and innovative work.

ART MUSEUM OF THE AMERICAS

201 18th Street NW, 202/458-6016, www.oas.org, click on museum, **Metro Stop:** Farragut West (blue and orange lines) and Farragut North (red line), Open Tuesday through Sunday 10am to 5pm, Closed Mondays, federal holidays and Good Friday, Admission: free.

Small and accessible, this cozy art museum opened in 1976 at the 200th anniversary of the independence of the United States. The Spanish Colonial mansion was designed in 1912 by noted architect Paul Cret as the residence of the Secretary General of the Organization of American States. The lovely red-tiled roof and loggia decorated with brilliantly colored tiles in patterns modeled after Aztec and Inca legends is a peaceful place to come to relax and take in some art.

Our children's favorite painting, unanimous choice, is Rufino Tamayo's *Man Contemplating the Moon*.

DECATUR HOUSE MUSEUM

748 Jackson Place NW, 202/842-0920, www.decaturhouse.org, **Metro Stop:** Farragut West (blue and orange lines) and Farragut North (red line), Open 10am to 5pm and Saturday and Sunday from noon to 4pm, Closed Mondays, Thanksgiving, December 25 and January, **Tours:** Tuesday through Friday, every half hour from 10am to 3pm and Saturdays and Sundays from noon to 4pm. Admission: free.

Location, location, location. The Decatur House was the first and last private residence located on Lafayette Square – basically a close neighbor of the President. It was designed in 1818 by Benjamin Henry Latrobe for navy hero Commodore Stephen Decatur. The prestigious location made this a popular home and many ambassadors, members of Congress and other dignitaries vied for ownership.

The museum has preserved the lives of the residents of Decatur House, particularly the Decatur and Beale families. The home has an intriguing history. Decatur and his young wife, Susan Wheeler, purchased the land and commissioned Latrobe, known as the nation's first architect, to design the home. Unfortunately, after only 14 months of living in their new home, Decatur was killed in a duel with Commodore James Baron. Susan packed up and moved into a smaller home in Georgetown, while maintaining ownership of the Decatur House. She rented the house to several secretaries of state, including Henry Clay and Martin Van Buren.

Charlotte Dupuy, a slave of Henry Clay, raised the stakes at the Decatur House by suing Clay for her freedom and that of her two children. Sadly, she lost her case before the U.S. Circuit Court of the District of Columbia, but finally gained her freedom 11 years later.

The museum currently has an exhibit on the slaves of Decatur House.

Time to Shop

This is the place to go if you want an elegant gift reminiscent of the early days of the U.S. government – Presidential china and White House Christmas ornaments to wonderful children's books, toys and games.

CORCORAN GALLERY OF ART

500 17th Street NW (near the Daughters of the American Revolution), 202/639-1700, www.corcoran.org, **Metro Stop:** Farraguat West (bluen and orange lines), Open daily, except Tuesday, 10am to 5pm, Thursday until 9pm,. Admission: $5 for individuals, $3 seniors and students, $1 students under 13-18, $8 family groups of any size, children under 12 free, **Tours;** Docent-led tours are available daily, except Tuesday, at noon, 7:30pm on Thursday and 2:30pm Saturday and Sunday.

The largest, non-federal art museum in Washington, D.C., the Corcoran Gallery of Art was founded in 1869 and is the city's first art museum. The permanent collection contains masterpieces from America and Europe.

Special exhibits often are innovative (multi-media presentations) and fascinating (Jacquline Kennedy).

Sundays are fun at the Corcoran. There is a brunch at the Café des Artiste with Jazz or Gospel music (Open 11am-2pm Sunday, 11am-2pm daily, except Thursday when it's open 11am to 8pm. Closed Tuesday). The Sunday brunch costs $21.95 for adults and $10.95 for children 10 and under. Children are welcome.

The gift shop has lovely art-related items, not as child friendly though as the Smithsonian art galleries nor the National Gallery.

OCTAGON MUSEUM

1799 New York Avenue (2 blocks west of White House), 202/638-3105, www.archfoundation.org, **Metro stop:** Farragut North (red line) and Farragut West (blue and orange lines), Open Tuesday through Sunday from 10-4. Closed Mondays, Thanksgiving, Christmas and New Years Day. Admission: $5 adults, $3 students and seniors. **Tours:** Every hour on the half hour

The Octagon, the museum of the American Architectural Foundation, is the oldest museum of architecture in the country. Its works focus on the federal period – about 1800/1830 – although special exhibits cover a wide range of architectural and design pieces.

The building itself is a model of historic preservation. You'll be drawn to the beauty of the circular foyer with its marble floor, the elegant stairway and the surprisingly vivid colors of this federal period home.

DOWNTOWN II: MCI CENTER & ENVIRONS

MCI CENTER

7th and F Streets, 202/628-3200, www.mcicenter.com, **Metro Stop:** Gallery Place.

Michael Joooooooordan! Having grown up in Chicago, Michael (of this book) remains a diehard Bulls fan. And, Luck be with him as he and Michael (of hoop fame) relocated to Washington, D.C. – at least Jordan did for awhile. This state-of-the-art sport and entertainment center seats 20,000 fans. The MCI Center is home to the Washington Wizards, women's basketball team, the Mystics, hockey's Washington Capitols and Georgetown University men's college basketball. The arena also holds concerts and other shows suitable for families.

For those too young to recall the wizardry of even an aging Jordan, stop into the Discovery Channel Destination store. Michael once took little Anthony

/ and at half-time stepped into this store. They didn't get back
believable toys, games, books in an interactive environment.

Besides the Discovery Channel Destination store, the MCI Center is home to Modell's, a sports store that sells official T-shirts of various teams.

Time to Eat

Lots of choices here: Velocity Grill, an upscale restaurant, Nick & Stef's Steakhouse and F Street Sports Bar, another upscale place to eat, drink and enjoy jazz on Thursdays. More fun for the kids, however, are the food service stations located all around the stadium – you know peanuts, crackerjacks and hot dogs.

CHINATOWN FRIENDSHIP ARCHWAY

Seventh and H Streets, **Metro Stop:** Gallery Place.

Brilliant colors and dancing dragons greet your entry under this stunning arch into Washington's Chinatown district. Although the Chinese population has diminished over the years, the neighborhood remains vibrant. Our children love to see the archway, every time noticing a different dragon. It would be fabulous anywhere, but it particularly stands out in a city comprised mainly of gleaming white marble, or red-bricked, federal-style structures.

Chinatown is a great place to stop for a bite to eat. (More on that in the **I'm Hungry** section). It is close enough to the Shakespeare Theater, Navy Memorial, National Building Museum, Museum of American Art, the National Portrait Gallery and the MCI Center. Several of our friends always make a jaunt from the Mall to Chinatown for dinner.

The annual Chinese New Year Parade is exhilarating, with a promenade of brightly dressed dancers, floats and, of course dragons.

NATIONAL PORTRAIT GALLERY

Eight and F Streets, 202/357-2700 (Smithsonian Information), www.npg.si.edu, **Metro Stop:** Gallery Place (red line, Ninth Street exit),

The National Portrait Gallery, a Smithsonian museum, is closed for renovation until July 4, 2006.

NATIONAL BUILDING MUSEUM

401 F Street NW, 202/272-2448, www.nbm.org, **Metro Stop:** Judiciary Square (red line, F Street exit), Open Monday through Saturday from 10am to 5pm and Sunday, 11am-5pm.

Our children's first experience at the National Building Museum was on a school field trip. Never did we think to bring them there. Well, they came home and could not stop exclaiming of the joys of the Building Museum. Hmm, we thought. So one lazy, hazy, Saturday afternoon, we trotted down to see what all the buzz was about. And, we stayed until the guards began locking the doors! You don't have to be an architect to go ga-ga over this museum.

Our children highly recommend a stop into the *Tools as Art* exhibit, from the collection of John Hechinger. This is a real "tool-de-force," as is the outdoor sculpture designed by David Stroymeyer, and named the same. This room is filled with gadgets galore, all assembled to make some sort of fantastic art exhibit. We all delighted in *Schools of Fishes,* where visegrips are magically transformed into schools of fish. This clever and humorous exhibit included fun pieces such as Stephen Hansen's *Man on a Limb* (what's wrong with this picture?) and *Saw Bird* by Mark Blumenstein. *Tools*, totally cool kinetic art, made our children literally jump for joy.

The building is grand. An exterior frieze that weaves around the building is a parade of Civil War military units (Casper Buber, 1834-1899). Civil engineer and U.S. Army General Montgomery Meigs designed the building in 1881. It was completed in 1887.

Sashay into the Great Hall and travel back to the days of the Italian Renaissance. You can see why many a Presidential Inaugural Ball are held in this stunning room. Eight colossal Corinthian columns line the room, with a sparkling fountain dancing in the center.

Make the time to visit this museum. It is kid friendly and unique; plus there is space outdoors to run around if the urge overwhelms your youngest of travelers.

Fun Fact: The Corinthian columns are among the tallest in the world, standing 75 feet tall, 8 feet in diameter and 25 feet in circumference.

Time to Eat
The café is more than adequate for a light lunch or snack. We ate at one of the small tables set outside the café and gazed upon the beauty of the Great Hall.

Time to Shop
Do not go to this gift shop first. You and your children will never leave. From mazes to magnets, this gift shop is a filled with toys, games and books that will delight children of all ages. We buy many birthday gifts here.

NATIONAL MUSEUM OF WOMEN IN THE ARTS
1250 New York Avenue NW (corner of New York and 13th Streets), 202/783-5000, www.nma.org, **Metro Stop:** Metro Center (red, blue, orange lines, 13th Street exit), Open Monday through Friday from 10am to 5pm and Sunday from noon to 5pm, **Tours:** Call ahead to reserve a family tour, usually

ay (202/783-7996). Fee is $7 for adults, $5 college students and ission: $5 for adults, $3 students with ID and seniors, free for ⌐ 18.
ents are more than special at the National Museum of Women in the Arts – they are awesome. Our children have delighted in the homespun works of Grandma Moses, been dazzled by the puppetry and costumes created by Julie Taymor (of Lion King fame) and thoroughly enjoyed the Rapunzel book displays in the Library and Research Center.

The permanent collection includes works by Georgia O'Keefe, Camille Claudel and Karen Frakenthaler. The collection includes a wide variety of art forms – photography, paintings, prints, silver work, sculpture and other media.

The museum also has a partnership with Girl Scouts of America, which includes a Women in the Arts patch. For more information call 1-800/222-7270 and ask for the Girl Scout Coordinator.

Elegantly appointed, the building's main floor centers on the Great Hall. Two marble staircases outline the room, and enormous chandeliers light the airy and spacious hall.

Time to Eat

The Mezzanine Café is open from 11:30am to 2:30pm. You dine overlooking the stunning Great Hall. Slightly more eloquent dining than typically expected in a museum.

Time to Shop

Small but nice, the museum shop has a fine selection of prints and posters. There are few children's books, but they are high-quality, lovely art books for kids.

FBI

Ninth Street and Pennsylvania Avenue NW, 202/324-3447, www.fbi.gov, **Metro Stop:** Metro Center (blue, red, orange lines). **Tours:** Suspended until further notice.

This was one of the most popular tours in D.C. Tourists were able to get a peek at the FBI crime lab, the Ten Most Wanted and a Special Agent would conclude the tour with a firearms demonstration.

The best you can do as of this writing, is visit the FBI web site at this address www.fbi.gov/fbinbrief/tour/tour2.html and travel on a virtual tour of the FBI.

FORD'S THEATER/LINCOLN MUSEUM

511 Tenth Street NW, 202/638-2941, www.fordtheater.org, **Metro Stop:** Metro Center (red and blue/orange lines, 11th Street exit), Gallery Place (red, green, yellow lines, G Street exit) and Archives/Navy Memorial (yellow

and green lines, exit Pennsylvania Avenue), **Tours:** Free, National Park Ranger-led tours are usually available between 9am and 5pm. Call 202/426-6924 for current information, **Talks:** 15-minutes long, these talks cover the history of Lincoln's assassination and the Theater, They are given every hour on the quarter of the hour – beginning at 9:15am and ending with the last talk at 4:15pm).

Yes, this is THE Ford's Theater, where President Lincoln was assassinated on April 14, 1865. It was renovated in 1968, with the President's box restored to look as it was on that tragic day.

The Ford Theater offers marvelous family entertainment, including Gilbert and Sullivan plays and Marcel Marceau (mime). It was at a Marcel Marceau performance, when my son desperately needed to find a bathroom during the oh-so-brief intermission. Somehow, in an attempt tò meet his needs, we stumbled on the Lincoln Museum, housed in the Ford Theater. There was the coat Lincoln wore the night he was shot by the actor John Wilkes Booth, and his top hat. The assassin's gun, editorial cartoons of the day and fascinating photos also were on display. Needless to say, I bribed Anthony to leave the museum, use the bathroom and quickly return to his seat (candy got him to leave the museum, and a major promise to return, which we did after the show).

Parent Tip

This is a don't-miss museum. Yes, it's small and a bit off the beaten track. But it sure does interest kids who also pick up a lot of history along the way.

Fun Fact: Roger Mudd, an active member of the Board of Trustees for Ford's Theatre, is related to Dr. Samuel Mudd, who was accused of helping Booth escape by setting an ankle Booth had broken.

PETERSON HOUSE

526 Tenth Street (Across the street from the Ford Theatre), 202/426-6830, **Metro Stop:** Metro Center (red and blue/orange lines, 11th Street exit), Gallery Place (red, green, yellow lines, G Street exit) and Archives/Navy Memorial (yellow and green lines, exit Pennsylvania Avenue), Open daily from 9am to 5pm. Closed December 25.

A dying President Lincoln was carried from the Ford Theatre to this house directly across the street. His wife, Mary Todd, and son Robert spent the night of April 14, 1865 in the front parlor. Lincoln lay gravely ill, and eventually succumbed, through the double doors in the back parlor, at the rear of the house.

NATIONAL AQUARIUM/DEPARTMENT OF COMMERCE

14th Street and Constitution Avenue NW, 202/482-2825, www.nationalaquarium.com (National Aquarium in the Department of Commerce building), **Metro Stop:** Federal Triangle (orange and blue lines), Open daily 9am to 5pm, last admission at 4:30pm, **Talks:** Daily at 2pm (Sharks on Monday, Wednesday and Saturday; Piranha on Tuesday, Thursday and Sunday; and Alligators on Friday). Admission: Adults (age 11 and up) $3; children ages 2-10, .75 cents; under 2, free.

If you can't get to Baltimore, the Department of Commerce offers the next best thing – sort of – in the National Aquarium. Located in the lower level of the Department of Commerce building, the National Aquarium is the oldest aquarium in the country. There are no dolphin shows or flashy exhibits. Instead, this is small and cozy alternative, complete with sharks, piranha, turtles, baby alligators and other remarkable species.

The staff is more than helpful and full of facts.

Another point of interest in the Commerce Building is the enormous census clock located in the lobby that notes the births, deaths, immigration and emigration of everyone in the United States. It gives an approximate total population count, every second. Sooo, Big Brother is watching.

Time to Eat

No food is allowed in the National Aquarium.

Time to Shop

There are many souvenirs to celebrate your visit to the National Aquarium, along with lots of stuffed animals, books and toys. Not the best gift shop in town, but serviceable.

FOGGY BOTTOM

What an awful name for a neighborhood – foggy bottom? What's so foggy about it? Also known as the West End, Foggy Bottom once was home to Irish, German and African American immigrants who worked in the nearby breweries, glass plants and city gas works. Located near the Potomac, we can only imagine how swampy the land here must have been. So why not Swampy Bottom? Oh well.

Foggy Bottom is home to the infamous Watergate – known for the Nixon conspiracy and the Monica Lewinsky escapade. Hmmm, foggy bottom?

There is a bright side to this neighborhood. It is home to the John F. Kennedy Center for the Performing Arts, has wonderful access to Rock Creek Park and its bike trails and the Potomac for boating. Foggy Bottom is nestled in between Georgetown and Dupont Circle.

KENNEDY CENTER

New Hampshire Avenue at Rock Creek Parkwa,. 202/467-4000, www.kennedy-center.org, **Metro Stop:** Foggy Bottom/George Washington University (blue line), Open 10am until one-half hour after the final performance. **Tours:** Monday through Friday from 10am to 5pm and Saturday and Sunday, 10am to 1pm. Call 202/416-8340 for more information.

"Our contribution to the human spirit," is how President John F. Kennedy described the arts. It is this spirit that embodies the Kennedy Center, the city's heart of artistic endeavors for people of all ages.

Thoughts of a major cultural center emerged in 1958 when President Dwight D. Eisenhower signed legislation creating a National Cultural Center. President Kennedy grabbed hold of the project, raising funds and appointing Jacqueline Kennedy and Mrs. Eisenhower as co-chairs. Two months after Kennedy's assassination in November 1963, Congress designated the National Cultural Center as a "living memorial" to the fallen President. Since then, it has been named the John F. Kennedy Center of the Performing Arts. The Kennedy Center opened its doors on September 8, 1971.

The Kennedy Center overlooks the banks of the Potomac. Often before or during the intermission of a program, we take our children outside on the wide terrace to take in the view (and let any wiggles ride free with the breeze!) Evening hours are splendid on the terrace. The lights from Georgetown twinkle and glimmer, reflected on the waters of the peaceful Potomac. On the other side, you can enjoy views of the Capitol, Washington Monument and Lincoln and Jefferson Memorials outlined against the night sky.

Tours of the Kennedy Center highlight the many treasures donated from around the world. One of the most spectacular rooms is The Grand Foyer. It's deep-red carpet illuminated by 18 Orrefors crystal chandeliers enhances the features of the famous Robert Berks sculpture of President John F. Kennedy. It is a huge bust of Kennedy, which one day our little boy, only three at the time and visiting the Kennedy Center for his first time, remarked on the largeness of Kennedy's head by comparing it with the size of his baby sister's head (which was large for her body).

Tours of the Kennedy Center will take you through the Hall of the States, which displays the flags of the states in the order by which they entered the Union, and the Hall of Nations, where flags of nations diplomatically recognized by the U.S. hang in alphabetical order.

Several theaters and the American Film Institute comprise the Kennedy Center. Of particular note for children is the Millennium Stage. The Millennium Stage was launched in 1997 as part of the Performing Arts for Everyone Initiative. Every day – that is every day, 365 days a year — at 6pm a free performance – music, dance, theater – takes place. So get there early for a good spot to enjoy theater for everyone! Check the web site at www.kennedy-center.org/programs/millennium for a schedule of upcoming events.

EINSTEIN STATUE

2201 C Street NW (outside of the National Academy of Sciences building), 202/334-2000, National Academy of Sciences is open from 9am to 5pm, **Metro Stop**: Foggy Bottom/George Washington University, blue line.

Wonderful photo-op. Your children nestled on the lap of Albert Einstein. Sculptor Robert Berks designed this lovely memorial to Einstein for the centennial of the great master's birth (1979). Einstein is seen sitting down with a celestial map as a reminder that the universe was Einstein's laboratory.

Take the time to admire the Foucault pendulum located inside the National Academy of Sciences. In early March, the Academy usually has on display the high school winners of the Westinghouse Science Talent Search program. Science rules.

DEPARTMENT OF STATE

2201 C Street, 202/647-3241. **Metro Stop:** Foggy Bottom/George Washington University (blue line), **Tours:** Reservations only. Call 202/647-3241 or fax at 202/736-4232, Tours of the Diplomatic Rooms run Monday through Friday only at 9:30am, 10:30am and 2:45pm. Closed on weekends and federal holidays. Children under 12 are not recommended to attend. No strollers, briefcases or backpacks are permitted and there is no place to store them.

Experience life as a diplomat as you tour these elegant rooms at the Department of State. Antiques abound, many collected by Jacqueline Kennedy

DUPONT CIRCLE

Bookstores, cafes, art galleries. Dupont Circle adds a different twist to this political town. Housed throughout its more residential streets are several treasures of museums for families to visit. It's hard to believe that the area was quite rural until after the Civil War. That's when money started to move in, and it's been that way ever since. Many of the grand mansions of Massachusetts Avenue still exit, but now they are owned by foreign embassies. Walk up and down Mass Ave., from Dupont Circle, and see if you can guess all the countries by their flags.

THE PHILLIPS COLLECTION

1600 21st Street NW, 202/387-2151, www.phillipscollection.org, **Metro Stop**: Dupont Circle (red line, Q Street exit) Open Thursday through Saturday from 10am to 5pm, extended hours on Thursday to 8:30pm and Sunday noon to 7pm. Closed Monday. Admission: $7.50 for adults, $4 for seniors over 62 and full-time students and free for children 18 and under. Special exhibits may cost more. Tours: Wednesdays and Saturdays at 2pm, no charge. Gallery talks run the first and third Thursday of every month at 12:30pm, no charge. One-hour tours are available Tuesday through Friday at 10am 11:30am, 2pm and 3pm. They are offered by appointment and cost: $9.50 for adults, seniors (62+) and students, $7. Call 202/387-2151 for more information.

Note: Check on the museum's rules for strollers and baby backpacks. For some time, they did not allow strollers, but did allow backpacks.

One of our favorite museums, the Phillips Collection is housed in a charming and cozy mansion, once the home of Duncan Phillips. The smallness makes it especially accessible to children.

Duncan Phillips was born in Pittsburgh, Pennsylvania, in 1886, moving to Washington, D.C. at the age of 10. He is the grandson of James Laughlin, co-founder of Jones and Laughlin Steel Company. After the untimely death of his father and brother, Phillips and his mother opened up two of the rooms in their home as the Phillips Memorial Gallery. The Phillips' goal was to create an intimate and comfortable surrounding to view masterpieces of the world's art. Their dreams come true in this art museum.

From Georgia O'Keeffe to Jacob Lawrence, from Van Gough to Renoir, the gallery is an artistic tour-de-force. Our children come time and again to gaze upon Renoir's *Luncheon of the Boating Party*. Every time they find a new detail or person in the painting. My kids, Anthony and Carravita, love making up stories about who the people in Renoir's *Luncheon of the Boating Party* are and what they are talking about. It's a fun conversation that maybe your children also will enjoy.

Parent Tip

Do request the Family Fun Pack at the information desk or by calling 202/387-2151,ext 216 ahead of your visit. This is one of the best guides for children to an art museum we have seen. It's colorful pages featuring many of the gallery's paintings provides tips on how to keep your children engaged while viewing the art. It also provides fun post-visit activities for children to keep them thinking about the masterpieces they have seen.

The Phillips offers other art adventures for you and your family:

Artful Evenings

Held every Thursday from 5pm to 8:30 pm, Artful Evenings present gallery talks and live jazz music. While we have seen few children at these events, our kids have enjoyed them immensely. There is a cash bar with light refreshments, but not much food to keep the youngsters satisfied. Admission is $5 per person. Sometimes our children get in free, other times they have had to pay. Apparently there is no set policy.

Sunday Concerts

Sunday afternoon concerts have been a mainstay at the Phillips since 1947. The concerts, classical, begin at 5pm and are free-of-charge, with first-come-first-serve seating. They are scheduled from September through May. Children who enjoy classical music will most enjoy these concerts – as will you!

Time to Eat

Our family thoroughly enjoys the cozy café located on the ground floor, next to the gift shop. Sandwiches, soup and scrumptious deserts are great for lunch or just a snack. Cappuccino and hot chocolate are favorites on cool days. Open Tuesday through Saturday from 10:45am to 4:30pm and Sundays from noon to 4:30pm.

Time to Shop

Small but excellent gift shop, with lots of fun birthday gift ideas for children. From innovative art supplies to lovely art books, take time to visit the gift shop. Remember to stop here first if you want to play the Treasure Hunt game. You buy postcards of artwork found in the museum, and you and your child search for the works of art during your visit.

WOODROW WILSON HOUSE

2340 S Street NW, 202/387-4062, www.woodrowwilsonhouse.org.

Open Tuesday through Sunday 10am to 4pm. Closed Mondays, Thanksgiving, Christmas and federal holidays. Admission: Adults $5, Seniors $4, students $2.50, children under 7 free. METRO Stop: Dupont Circle

This was the final home for America's 28th president. Built in 1915 by architect Waddy Wood (sooo Roaring Twenties of a name!), the Georgian revival-style home has been carefully preserved to give you a glimpse of Wilson's last years in D.C.

Throughout the home, you will find treasures from the White House, including his wife's, Edith Wilson, White House portrait. You also will discover gifts from foreign dignitaries and more personal family items. You'll revel in flapper dresses from the Roaring Twenties and silent films.

A one-hour tour of the home includes a short film.

Time to Shop

Not surprisingly, the gift shop offers a host of items regarding Woodrow Wilson and the times he lived in. You can also find puzzles, cards, little gifts for little kids and fun cookbooks of the era.

FUN FACT: President Woodrow Wilson received the No₁ 1920 for his efforts to negotiate peace during World War 1. H. recall Wilson's 1918 Fourteen Points of Peace.

TEXTILE MUSEUM

2320 S Street NW, 202/667-0441, www.textilemuseum.org, ₥eetro Stop: Dupont Circle (redline, Q Street exit), Open Monday through Saturday 10am to 5pm and Sunday from 1pm to 5pm. Closed all federal holidays and December 25. Admission: Free, with a suggested donation of $5, Tours: Highlight Tours are from September through May, Wednesday, Saturday, Sunday at 1:30pm.

No one in our family is even close to being a home economics major. Nor are we Martha Stewart wannabes. So what are we doing visiting the Textile Museum? Going where our children dragged us after they visited on a field trip. What a delight!! This museum has gorgeous displays of ancient cloth and clothing from around the world. Exotic suits from Persia to Africa , we all were intrigued with how the sense of fashion merged with tradition and purpose. The museum's collection spans 5,000 years

Fun Fact: The Textile Museum was founded in 1925 by George Hewitt Myers with a collection of nearly 300 rugs and 60 related textiles.

The highlight of our trip was a visit to the Learning Center – totally interactive and informative. We all learned about fibers in their various stages of processing – from silk worm cocoons to silk thread. This is a touch-me, feel-me room where you learn about fabric, patterns and ancient customs. Have fun.

NATIONAL GEOGRAPHIC'S EXPLORERS' HALL

17ᵗʰ and M Street NW, 202/857-7788, www.nationalgeographic.com/ explorer, Metro Stop: Farragut North (red line) and Farragut West (blue line), Open Monday through Saturday and holidays 9am to 5pm and Sunday 10am to 5pm, Closed Christmas

Like the magazine, National Geographic's Explorers' Hall is alluring. The changing exhibits always are interactive, educational and daring. A trip to

Parent Tip

Come for Passport Fridays. Explorers' Hall comes alive with jumpn' music and presentations – most perfect for adventurous children – and adults. Call 202/857-7788 or visit www.nationalgeographic.com/ex-plorer/events.

☙

plorers' Hall will make you wonder why you didn't think of treking 3,200 kilometers across Africa with Michael Fey or travel to Niger with Dr. Paul Seranus to uncover the bones of the largest crocodile ever. Anthony, who played Captain Hook in his school play, was glad his crocodile-acting class-mate, Duncan, didn't have jaws that large!

Step outside to find the 5.5 meter high aluminum cast of a 7,000-year-old giraffe found in Niger.

B'NAI B'RITH KLUTZNICK NATIONAL JEWISH MUSEUM

1640 Rhode Island Avenue NW, 202/857-6583, www.bnaibrith.org, Metro Stop: Farragut West (red line) and Farragut North (blue line), Open Sunday through Friday from 10am to 5pm, Closed Saturday and , federal holidays and all Jewish holidays.

The B'nai B'rith Kluztnick National Jewish Museum, established in 1957, houses one of the most prestigious collections of Jewish art and artifacts in the United States. Located in the ground floor of the headquarters of B'nai B'rith International, a few blocks from the White House, the Museum presents exhibitions related to Jewish history and culture from antiquity to the present day. Collections relating to B'nai B'rith, the country's first Jewish social service organization, are also permanently on view.

The museum's permanent collection features the Horwitz collection of Judaica, containing Jewish artifacts, ceremonial art and folk art from the Biblical period through the current day.

NORTHWEST D.C.

NATIONAL ZOO

3001 Connecticut Avenue NW, 202/637-4950, www.fonz.org, **Metro Stop**: Woodley Place (red line) or Cleveland Park (red line), Open May 1 to September 15 6am to 8pm, buildings open from 10am to 6pm. From September 16 to April 30 from 6am to 6pm, buildings from 10am to 4:30pm.

Anthony and Carravita spent their baby and toddler years living two blocks from the zoo. We often listened to the lions roar in the early hours around dawn. Later in the morning, the sound of gibbons howling greeted us – their haunting, hoot-hoot-hooting sounds echoing throughout the zoo and our neighborhood. Our little ones learned to ride their little bikes on the road, part of Rock Creek Park, that circles the zoo. Oh yes, and wintertime brought shouts and cheers when we pulled out their sleds to ride recklessly down Lion Hill.

Note: The National Zoo is situated on a steep, steep hill. Be prepared. If your little ones need assistance, you can rent strollers at any information kiosk for $7 for a single and $10 for a double stroller. Do remember how hot D.C.

can get. The National Zoo thoughtfully provides sprinklers at key spots up and down the main path through the zoo. Children and big people enjoy getting doused with a light drizzle on those oh-so-hot days.

I'm sure your family has its menagerie of favorite animals and zoo exhibits. Here is a top-ten list of what to see at the National Zoo, thanks to Anthony, Carravita and their friends Katheen and Sam:

10. Kids' Farm. The latest addition to the National Zoo, Kids' Farm shows children what farms are about and how we get food from farms (No, Paris and Nickie are not tour guides here). Enjoy petting and grooming goats and donkeys and getting up close to other animals at the Caring Corral. Make sure you see the pizza "garden." The farm folks at the National Zoo use the ingredients of pizza to help children discover how food used in pizza grows.

9. Bats in the belfry!! Enter the bat cave, if you dare. Located under Lion Hill is a dark, cavern filled with bats. Don't worry. They are behind a glass window, and actually are quite cute.

8. The birds, the birds. They fly overhead or cozy up into trees at the Bird House. Check out the Bird House resource room – open 10am to 2pm Saturday and Sunday, 10am to noon Monday through Friday. Right outside the Bird House are two ponds with an assortment of ducks and swans.

7. Komodo dragons can be found at the Reptile House. Outside, my daughter loves to look for alligators and crocodiles skimming the surface of their watery homes.

6. Cheetahs. Sleek and graceful, these endangered animals are mesmerizing to watch. Check at the information desk for times they are fed. A video on research the National Zoo is engaged in to help get the cheetahs off the endangered list runs non-stop next to their area.

5. Golden lion tamarins. These monkeys can be found roaming the Valley Trail and nearby areas. Be prepared to patiently scan the surrounding area in search for the tamarins.

4. The Great Apes. The Great Apes include gorillas, orangutans and gibbons. We have always found the gorilla families most majestic, and often wonder who's looking at whom. Look overhead for the orangutans, as they may be crossing the O-line – a sort of tightrope – from their home to the Think Tank. Great Ape interpreters are available to answer questions on Wednesday 10am to 1pm and Thursday through Sunday 10am to 4pm.

3. The Think Tank. A unique zoo experience, the Think Tank is not so much an exhibit as a research center that allows visitors in on the work of scientists. The Think Tank's purpose is to explore the concept of thinking. Numerous exhibits on animal thinking are peppered throughout the Think Tank. But, you can also view scientists studying the orangutans' or macaques' thinking process and ability to use their minds to socialize and pass on social rules.

2. Seals and Sea Lions. Anthony, Carravita and their friends could stand for hours at the back end of the seal tank where a window gives you a glance of the seals' underwater antics. What fun to watch the seal training held daily at 11:30.

1. Amazonia. A rainforest exhibit that grips you into believing you're actually roaming the forest. See the many fish that inhabit the waters of the rainforest. Once upstairs, search skyward for signs of the sloth and colorful rainforest birds. Amazonia is the most species-rich exhibit at the zoo, with not only animals, birds and reptiles, but over 2, 500 fish! Then, walk over to the field station of the fictitious Dr. Brasil to peek at the exotic-colored poison-dart frogs. Stop in during the fish feeding demonstration (Fridays at 11am)

Adjacent to Amazonia is the Science Gallery where you can peer into microscopes, keep a watch via a computer system on the status of earthquakes around the globe, examine an exotic butterfly collection and watch real scientists at work. Amazonia and the Science Gallery are great rainy day trips. Both are indoors and thoroughly engage children for quite a long time.

Parent Tip

Spend a Thursday evening at the Zoo for the Sunset Serenade. These free, outdoor concerts on Lion/Tiger Hill run from 6:30pm until 8pm. Bring a blanket and a picnic dinner, or buy food at the Zoo. Sit back and relax or dance along with the music! These are popular events scheduled from the end of June to the beginning of August.

ROCK CREEK PARK

Located throughout Washington, D.C.

The hustle bustle of life in the capitol city gently fades as citizens and visitors alike step into the lush greenery of Rock Creek Park. Bubbling creeks, cascading falls, stone bridges soothe the souls of all who take the time to enjoy all that Rock Creek Park has to offer. Trails for hiking, fields for soccer, bike paths, tennis courts, horseback riding and picnic groves – Rock Creek has it all, and more.

History abounds in the Park. Follow the path of the Algonquin Indians. Visit Peirce Mill and the Old Stone House to see what life was like when this city was just beginning to spread its wings.

Fun Fact: Rock Creek Park, created in 1890 and running about 2,000 acres, is the oldest urban park administered by the National Park Service.

Before children, we used the Park to bike to work and for pleasure over the weekend. On Saturday, Sunday and holidays, several main car roads running through the Park are closed to traffic, giving bicyclists, runners, roller bladers and strollers control of the road. On one early, early morning jog through the Park, we noticed a huge and beautiful cat keeping an eye on us. Wiping groggy eyes, we soon realized that was no cat, but a beautiful gray fox. The park is home to foxes (more red than grey), deer and raccoon.

Fun Fact: At last count, Rock Creek Park was home to 85 whitetail deer and about 8 fox dens. The Park is purported to have the largest density of raccoon in the United States. So, do remember it is their home, too. Keep the park clean and please do not pick any of the flowers or other shrubs.

Here are some of the fun family adventures you can have at Rock Creek Park:

Nature Center, 5200 Glover Road NW, 202/426-6828 or 6829, www.nps.gov/rocr/naturecenter, **Metro Stop:** Friendship Heights (red line), then take the E-2 or E-3 bus to the intersection of Military Road and Glover. Look to your left and follow the trail up to the Nature Center. Open Wednesday through Sunday 9am to 5pm, Closed New Year's Day, Fourth of July, Thanksgiving and Christmas.

Children are warmly welcomed at the Nature Center, and have been throughout its history. The Nature Center opened its doors on June 4, 1960. Today, visit the center to see an observation beehive and the hands-on Discovery Room where puppets, books and other activities help children develop an awareness and appreciation of the natural world. Or take a guided nature walk, led by the quite friendly and amazingly knowledgeable Park Rangers. For young children or those stroller-bound, there is a short, well-paved nature walk – The Edge of the Woods Trail — right outside the doors of the Nature Center – a favorite when our children were younger. For a more slightly strenuous hike, try the short Woodlands Trail.

Exhibit Hall is overflowing with plant and animal life indigenous to Rock Creek Park. Pick up the activity sheets that will guide your child through Exhibit Hall and see how much you can learn in a short time!

The Nature Center has daily programs to delight nature lovers of all ages. Fridays at 4pm Park Rangers introduce children to the many animals who reside in the park. The Nature Center also is home to the **Planetarium** (202/426-6829, www.nps.gov/rocr/planterium). The only planetarium in the National Park System, the Planetarium duplicates the motion of the stars and planets using a Spitz planetarium projector. Several shows are available: After-School Planetarium Program (Wednesday at 4pm). On Saturday and Sunday at 1pm, The Night Sky, is shown. It is an introduction to the night sky aimed for children four and older. Later at 4pm is a program for children 7 and older. Free tickets are available 1/2 hour before the show.

Near to the Nature Center are the horse stables, where you can go **horseback riding.** One-hour guided tours cost $25. Younger children, who must be at least 30 inches tall, can go on pony rides for $10. Call 202/362-0118 for more details.

Peirce Mill, on Tilden Drive between Connecticut and Beech, 202/426-6908, www.nps.gov/rocr/piercemill, **Metro Stop**: Cleveland Park (red line, exit Connecticut Avenue East) then walk two blocks north, on the right side of the street, hike down the 1/2 mile, downhill Melvin Hazin trail, at the bottom, turn left and cross Tilden Street to the Mill. Open Wednesday through Sunday from 10am to 5 pm. Closed Monday and Tuesday.

After a stint in America's Revolutionary War, Issac Peirce left his Quaker home in Pennsylvania, seeking fortune in Maryland by working for Abner Cloud, a millwright. He married Cloud's daughter, Betsy, and soon after Maryland ceded square miles to form the new Capitol City. Peirce's fortunes continued to soar. His Peirce Plantation included an old mill that Peirce and his son Abner rebuilt during the 1820s. The stone mill incorporates many of the innovative devices conceived by Oliver Evans from Delaware to make mills run with less manpower needed.

In the 1880s, new steam-powered mills made the Peirce Mill obsolete. Congress' decision to preserve Rock Creek Valley as a national park perhaps saved Peirce Mill from demolition. Today, it is a picturesque reminder of the past and a charming picnic spot for families. We often bike with our children to Peirce Mill, enjoye a snack, spend time tossing small stones into the creek, and watch – at a distance – the thundering waterfall. Visit the **Art Barn** next to the mill and shop for unique gifts made by local artists. A lovely afternoon at Peirce Mill.

GEORGETOWN

Georgetown. Remember the scene from Peter Pan when Michael, Wendy and John must think lovely thoughts in order to fly? Fishing, hopscotch, candy! And little John can think only of candy? Well, in Georgetown, thinking lovely thoughts turns into shopping – and more shopping! From the hip to the avant-garde, boutiques abound in Georgetown. There even is a mall – an incredibly upscale, splendid mall.

Georgetown also is the home of Georgetown University, tree-lined residential streets filled with mostly narrow, brick row houses. It is a town within a city – where scores of celebrities lived and still live, from Madeline Albright to Elizabeth Taylor, from John F. Kennedy to Averil Harrimon.

Besides shopping, there are several historical sites to visit. First stop, we recommend the Old Stone House.

OLD STONE HOUSE

3051 M Street NW, 202/426-6851, www.nps.gov/rocr/olst, Open Wednesday through Sunday 10am to 5pm, Closed New Year's Day, July Fourth, Thanksgiving and Christmas.

The oldest house left standing in Washington, D.C. is the Old Stone House. History comes to life upon a visit to the house, which offers weary travelers a pleasant rest time in the gardens.

In 1764, Rachel and Christopher Laymen and their two sons migrated from Pennsylvania to the port town of Georgetown. For one pound, ten shillings they purchased property to build their one-room home made of blue fieldstone quarried just two miles up river. Just one year later, Christopher died unexpectedly and Rachel eventually sold the house to Cassandra Chew. Cassandra, a prominent Georgetown landowner, promptly renovated the house, adding a second floor between 1767 and 1775. Upon her death in 1807, Cassandra passed the house on to her daughter, Mary Smith Brumley.

In 1953, the federal government bought the home for $90,000 in response to a strong neighborhood association that claimed the house had historical significance. Over the years, the home was restored and the English garden added.

The tour of the house is short and sweet – a nice break from your Georgetown shopping spree. And, if little ones are, hmm, shall we say not quite swept up with the historical significance of the house, you can quickly exit to the garden for a breath of fresh air and a game of I Spy.

Fun Fact: Prior to the federal government purchasing the home in 1953, the garden was nothing more than a paved lot where a car dealership, Parkway Motor Company, parked its cars.

C &O CANAL AND BARGE RIDES

1057 Thomas Jefferson Street NW, 202/653-5190, www.nps.gov/choh.

The C & 0 Canal is a fabulous recreational area, overflowing with historical tales. Visitor centers are located along the park in Georgetown, Great Falls Tavern, Brunswick, Williamsport, Hancock and all the way to Cumberland, Maryland.

You can hike, bike or, what fun, ride the historical canal boats. The boat rides, which are offered at two locations along the canal, transport passengers back in time. Park Rangers dress in 19th-century clothing as they describe the history of the canal. Prices are $8 for adults and $5 for children. For more information, visit the Georgetown visitor center at 1057 Thomas Jefferson Street NW, 202/653-5190. Call also to learn more about ranger-led tours, which focus on the park's natural and cultural resources.

Fun Fact: The Chesapeake and Ohio Canal is 184.5 miles long, stretching from Washington, D.C. to Cumberland, Maryland. Initial plans called for the canal to reach Pittsburgh, but it never did. The canal operated as a major transportation route between 1828 and 1924. Floods and railroads were the demise of the canal as a transportation route.

DUMBARTON OAKS

1703 32 Street NW, , 202/339-6410, www.doaks.org, Open March 15 to October 2 from 2pm to 6pm. Admission: $5 adults and $3 children and seniors. It is also open from November 14 through March from 2pm to 5pm. Admission then is free. Tours: Docent-led tours are available, but you must call ahead.

Enchanting gardens embrace this splendid Federal-style home. The original home was purchased by Mr. And Mrs. Robert Woods Bliss and in 1940, they gave their home and art collection to Harvard University.

We often visit the gardens with paper and crayons in hand. Children enjoy sketching the sundry flowers and plants. After awhile, they like to play imaginary games frolicking – no running, please – throughout the numerous paths. It's a delightful afternoon.

Check at the information booth for a brochure that describes the history of the building and gardens and describes the many plants and flowers.

FRANCIS SCOTT KEY PARK & THE STAR-SPANGLED BANNER MONUMENT

35th and M Street NW, 202/333-2041.

Snuggled next to the Georgetown end of the Key Bridge is a quaint little park dedicated to Francis Scott Key, writer of the Star-Spangled Banner. Key lived in a house quite near this park. During the 1600s, the land here was occupied by several Indian tribes, including the Potomacks. Now it is an oasis of greenery in the midst of the fast-paced Georgetown neighborhood.

From the park, look across and see Virginia. In the center of the park is a bronze bust of Francis Scott Key, and a lighted flagpole flies the 15-star, 15-stripe flag of Key's day.

UPPER NORTHWEST

U.S. NAVAL OBSERVATORY

Massachusetts Avenue and Observatory Circle, 202/762-1467, www.usno.navy.mil.

Public tours of the Observatory have re-opened and are offered on alternating Monday evenings from 8:30pm until 10:00pm, except on Federal holidays. Our children love this tour, which a viewing of celestial objects with

the 12-inch Alvan Clark refractor with an astronomer. You mu
either on-line or by fax at 202/762-1489. Make your request
six weeks in advance. You must include the names and dates
individuals in your party, a daytime telephone number and/c
address so that we may contact you with the status of your reques.   ours do
fill up and are subject to elimination at any time.

The Observatory is responsible for keeping time. What? Well, keeping time is actually more difficult than you think. Several master clocks are kept in separate climate-controlled environments to determine the exact, up-to-the-minute time. When tours resume, the rest of the visit will focus on astronomy and a chance to view the night sky through the Observatory's powerful telescope.

NATIONAL CATHEDRAL

Massachusetts and Wisconsin Avenues, 202/364-6616, www.cathedral.org, **Metro Stop**: Tenleytown (red line, exit west side of Wisconsin, then take any 30 series bus going south) or from Dupont Circle take one of these buses: N2, N3, N4, N6 to the corner of Massachusetts and Wisconsin, the Cathedral is one-half block north. Tours: Docent-led tours are offered Sunday from 12:45pm to 2:30, Monday through Friday from 10am to 11:30pm and from 12:45pm to 3:15pm and Saturday from 10am to 11:30pm and from 12:45 to 3:15 (the nave often is closed on Saturday due to special events at the church) . Other tours are described below.

One day while Carravita was playing with a friend, Anthony (age 9 at the time) and Barbara on a whim decided to visit the National Cathedral and, equally unexpectedly signed up for the regular docent-led tour. Barbara figured she could always leave if Anthony became jumpy and restless. How exciting can a tour of a cathedral be? Well, climbing almost into the rafters and close enough to see the inside of the bell tower was more than enough to keep Anthony engaged. Fear of heights? Look out, because you truly get a bird's eye view of the church on this tour. Anthony even found interesting the many stories behind the stained glass windows scattered throughout the church,

Parent Tip

Gargoyles peer hauntingly from the rafters of this great cathedral – and children just can't get enough. Well, here's a tour your little ones won't moan and groan about. A gargoyle tour of the cathedral is available for children from April through October. You will see a slide show all about these creepy critters and learn about their creation. Next you'll go on a walk to find some of them – before they find you!! Call 202/537-2934 for information and reservations.

although more interesting were the lightening rods the guide showed us when we were ushered outside – and way up – to take in the view.

Fun Fact: This is too cool. Leave the Cathedral at the northwest corner of the nave, through the double wooden doors of Lincoln Bay. Walk down the ramp and into the parking lot. Turn around and look up at the tower closest to you. Use binoculars. There, way up is – can it be? – Darth Vadar staring down. A competition was held through National Geographic Magazine for children to design a decorative sculpture for the Cathedral. Christopher Radar was one of the winners, with his sketch of the evil Vadar.

Plenty of summer afternoons we have all spent in the splendid **gardens** of the Cathedral – reading stories, coloring, playing I Spy and even a slow and calm hide-and-seek. The gardens are surrounded by a small wood, just perfect for children to explore and discover. Often we take a snack and picnic in the small field behind the Bishop's Rose Garden. A great spot after a long day of touring. Don't forget to look for the goldfish pond!

The National Cathedral was conceived in 1893 when Congress granted a charter to the Protestant Episcopal Cathedral Foundation of the District of Columbia to allow the creation of a cathedral. After being anointed the first bishop of Washington in 1896, Reverend Dr. Henry Yates Satterlee secured land on Mount Saint Alban. The foundation stone was laid in 1907. And with that stone came the longest-running construction site in the nation's capitol. It wasn't until the completion of the west towers in 1990 that the Cathedral was considered complete.

Fun Facts: More than 150 people are interred in the Cathedral, including Woodrow Wilson and Helen Keller.

How many angels playing various instruments do you think are adorned on the west towers? 320.

The National Cathedral is the sixth-largest cathedral in the world, the second-largest in the U.S. Only St. John's in New York City is larger in the U.S.

What is a gargoyle, really? It actually serves as a gutter intended to carry rain water away from the walls and foundations. There are 110 gargoyles standing guard –looking for rain – around the Cathedral.

Besides the gargoyle tour mentioned in the Parent Tip, the National Cathedral has other family friendly activities. Family Saturday events often are scheduled. One recent event was a Teddy Bear Tea and Tour for children age 4 to 11. Carravita and Barbara signed up and had a great time learning about the animals in all the stained glass windows and elsewhere. The tea in the Pilgrim Observation Gallery was only topped off by the spectacular view of D.C.

Lord of the Rings lovers will find the Medieval Workshops almost as exciting as the Hobbit adventures. These workshops are held in the Cathedral's crypt. Children experience carving a piece of limestone, working on an anvil, creating a clay gargoyle or grotesque, illuminating a manuscript and other activities, while learning about the life and culture of the Middle Ages. The workshops are held Saturday from 10am to 2pm. Cost is $5. Call 202/537-2934 for more information.

Time to Shop

The Museum Store is housed in the basement and offers both religious and non-religious items ranging from jewelry, sculpture and art work to books, music and posters. The children's book section has a marvelous selection of books about all religions and with spiritual themes. Lovely stained glass artwork abounds.

The Herb Cottage, located between the Cathedral and the gardens is open from 10am to 5pm daily (202/537-8982.) Here you can acquire outdoor statues, jams, herbs, table linens and cute cuddlies.

The Greenhouse sells, not surprisingly, flowers and plants. We always buy our supply of annuals and perennials here. The staff is on top of the gardening game, most helpful and kind. The Greenhouse is open Tuesday through Saturday from 9:30am to 5pm and Sunday from 10am to 5pm. Call 202/537-6263 for information on their gardening lecture series.

Time to Eat

Delightful biscuits, cookies, crackers and even sandwiches can be found in the Museum Store. Great treats to nibble on across the way in the gardens.

SOUTHEAST D.C.

FREDERICK DOUGLASS NATIONAL HISTORIC SITE

1411 W Street SE, 202/426-5961, www.nps.gov/frdo/freddoug Open April to October from 9am to 5pm and from October through March from 9am to 4pm. Admission: free if you come by **Tourmobile** or are in a group of 4 or less and $2 per person if you don't come on the Tourmobile. Tours: Guided tours are the only way in. They run about 45 minutes and are scheduled at 9am, 10, am, 11am, 1pm, 2pm, and 3pm and 4pm, during the months the home is open until 5pm. To reserve a tour for five or more, call 800/967-2283.

Frederick Douglass – a Renaissance man. Douglas was an abolitionist, publisher of the North Star newspaper, presidential appointee and the first black to break the racial ban on homeownership in what is now Anacostia, a D.C. neighborhood.

Douglas paid $6,700 in 1877 for this stunning, 21-room, white brick Victorian home. Your tour guide will point out the desk and chair given to Douglass by Harriet Beecher Stowe (author of Uncle Tom's Cabin) and

President Lincoln's cane bequeathed to Douglass by Mary Lincoln. The grounds are expansive enough for a romp around or a quiet time in the little garden with footbridge. We also enjoyed seeing the tiny replica of Douglass' writing retreat.

Check out the short film of his life. Our children and their friends, David (12) and Atena (9), enjoyed the acting and real life portrayals in the film. All the children were quite impressed with the fact that Douglass chose to learn, since as a slave he was not allowed to attend school, and worked hard at educating himself so he could reach his potential and accomplish great things. However, we all agree that someone should paint his house, the outside is fast chipping away. Any fundraisers out there?

ANACOSTIA MUSEUM AND CENTER FOR AFRICAN AMERICAN HISTORY AND CULTURE

1901 Fort Place SE, 202/287-2060 (recording) or 202/287-3306, www.si.edu/anacostia, Transportation: The best way to get to the museum is to take the Anacostia Shuttle, which operates Monday-Friday in the afternoons form the National Mall. For the shuttle schedule, check at any of the Smithsonian Museums information or call the Smithsonian at 202/357-2700 Open every day from 10am to 5pm, Closed Christmas.

The Anacostia Museum is the Smithsonian Institution's museum of African-American history and culture. The museum explores America's history, society and creative endeavors through the perspective of African Americans.

A recent exhibit focused on African American writers, including Charles Johnson, author of Middle Passage, a highly acclaimed novel of the horrifying slave trade. Our children, along with their friends David and Atena, sat mesmerized at the video of Johnson reading from his book. And, they enjoyed seeing hand-edited version of his book. The children particularly enjoyed seeing an exhibit on Eloise Greenfield, the children's author.

WASHINGTON NAVY YARD

Building 76, 805 Kidder Breese SE, 202/433-4882, **Metro Stop:** Eastern Market (blue or orange line, exit Pennsylvania Avenue SE, then walk six blocks down 8th Street to the Yard or take bus number 90 or 92 on 8th Street), Open Monday through Friday from 9am to 4pm, closed weekends and Thanksgiving, Christmas Eve and Day, and New Year's Day. Tours: You must call in advance to schedule any tour and have an ID card for anyone over age 18.

Ahoy, there mates. This is the Captain speaking. The Navy Museum is the place to go for old salts and land lubbers alike. Exhibits of ship models, uniforms, medals, paintings – all about the Navy and the sea. There are gun mounts to climb on and periscopes to peer through.

Perhaps the most fun is touring the U.S.S. Barry, anchored on tı. Anacostia River. The Barry is a decommissioned Navy destroyer. Oh, the pleasures a child has marching around the ship, stepping into the galley, mess hall, engine room and officers quarters.

Time to Eat

Here are several options for eating in the Navy Yard;

Building 200 Food Court (Subway Sandwich Shop, Dunkin' Donuts, and Friendly's Ice Cream), open weekdays from 6am to 5pm, 202/889-8800.

Building 36, William III Snack Bar (Sandwiches, gourmet coffee and pastries), open weekdays from 6:30am to 2:30pm, (202) 889-2378

Building 184, McDonalds, open weekdays from 5:30am to 5pm and Saturday during the summer from 9am to 3pm, 202/889-3085

Picnic tables are scattered around the Museum and throughout the Navy Yard if you wish to picnic outdoors.

Chapter 7

JUST OUTSIDE D.C.

NEARBY VIRGINIA

Nearby means directly across the Potomac! The short span of a bridge is all that separates the Lincoln Memorial, in Washington, from Arlington Cemetery, in Arlington, Virginia. From there, a drive southwest along the Potomac River takes you through Old Town Alexandria on your way to George Washington's historic home at Mt. Vernon. So, do take the time to cross the river and enjoy what nearby Virginia has to offer.

ARLINGTON CEMETERY

West side of Memorial Bridge, 703/697-2131, www.arlingtoncemetery.org, **Metro Stop:** Arlington National Cemetery, Tourmobile Stop. Open April 1 to September 30 from 8am to 7pm daily and from October through March from 8am to 5pm daily.

A few years after President Kennedy was laid to rest, Barbara's eighth-grade field trip to Washington descended upon America's capitol. Visiting the gravesite was a highlight of the trip, a shocking reminder to young people of the fragility of life, even for the high and mighty. It is a somber recollection. Your children will not share the anguished memories of that day, as many of us parents do, but they will sense the strength and spirituality that blankets this national cemetery.

Rows upon rows of white-stone markers stand at attention throughout the cemetery, marking the multitude of soldiers who have lost their lives defending the country. More than 220,000 war dead are buried in the 612 acres of gently rolling hills. So are many of America's celebrities – from Joe

Louis to JFK. Do get a map at the Visitors Center to help guide your way through the cemetery, or take the TOURMOBILE, which makes many stops so you can get off and on to visit the sites of most interest to you.

Here are several highlights of the trip, the graves of: President John F. Kennedy and Jacqueline Kennedy Onasiss, Senator Robert Kennedy, Joe Louis, Secretary of State John Foster Dulles, Oliver Wendell Holmes, Supreme Court Justice Thurgood Marshall, Admiral Hyman G. Rickover, President William Howard Taft.

Fun Fact: Did you know that three of the first five presidents of the U.S. died on July 4? Thomas Jefferson, John Adams and James Monroe.

Do make it over to the **Tomb of the Unknown Soldier**. The changing-of-the-guard ceremony is elegant and somber — a truly moving experience. Members of the 3rd Infantry Regiment from Fort Meyer stand guard day and night over the white marble sarcophagus. Sculpted into the east panel of the sarcophagus are the words: Peace, Victory and Valor. The changing-of-the-guard takes place every half-hour from April through September and every hour on the hour from October through March.

The story of the Unknown Soldier is one worth telling: On Memorial Day in 1921 four unknown soldiers were exhumed from graves in France. Highly decorated U.S. Army Sgt. Edward F. Younger, who was wounded in combat, was chosen to choose which of the unknown soldiers would make the journey back to America to represent all unknown soldiers. Younger made his selection by placing a spray of white roses on the third casket from the left. This casket was carried back to the United States, while the others were interred in the Meuse Argonne Cemetery in France.

Initially, the Unknown Soldier lay in state in the Capitol Rotunda from his arrival in the United States until Armistice Day, 1921. On Nov. 11, 1921, President Warren G. Harding officiated at the interment ceremonies at the Memorial Amphitheater at Arlington National Cemetery. Thus began a military tradition.

On Aug. 3, 1956, President Dwight D. Eisenhower signed a bill to select and pay tribute to the unknowns of World War II and Korea. Navy Hospitalman 1st Class William R. Charette, then the Navy's only active-duty Medal of Honor recipient, selected the Unknown Soldier of World War II in 1958. Army Master Sgt. Ned Lyle made the final selection among the deceased of the Korean War.

The Unknown service member from the Vietnam War was designated by Medal of Honor recipient U.S. Marine Corps Sgt. Maj. Allan Jay Kellogg Jr. during a ceremony at Pearl Harbor, Hawaii, May 17, 1984. Interestingly, the remains of the Vietnam Unknown were exhumed May 14, 1998. Based on mitochondrial DNA testing, Department of Defense scientists identified the remains as those of Air Force 1st Lt. Michael Joseph Blassie, who was shot down near An Loc, Vietnam, in 1972. A decision was made to keep vacant the crypt that contained the remains of the Vietnam Unknown.

Parent Tip

Bring water, lots of it, if you're visiting Arlington Cemetery on one of Washington's notoriously hot, steamy summer days. The heat can be choking in the Cemetery, where there is little shade.

Here are several of the many other monuments you may be interested in visiting while at the cemetery, beginning with the home of Robert E. Lee:

ARLINGTON HOUSE

Set high on a hill, with a panoramic view of Washington, is the Arlington House, once the mansion of Civil War General Robert E. Lee. On a visit to the Arlington House, President John F. Kennedy, taking in the view, was overheard wistfully saying, "I could stay here forever." His grave, and those of his brother Robert and wife Jacqueline Kennedy Onassis, as well as two of their infant children, are buried just steps away.

Arlington House is open all year from 9:30am to 4:30pm. The Arlington House/Robert E. Lee Museum is open from 8am to 4:30pm. Arlington House ground are open from 8am to 7pm between April 1 and September 30, and from 8am to 5pm between October 1 and March 31. Arlington House, Grounds and Museum are closed December 25th and January 1st.

MARINE CORPS MEMORIAL (IWO JIMA)

Located at the north end of the cemetery near the Orde-Weitzel Gate stands the statue of marines raising the flag over Iwo Jima – now made more haunting by the 9-11 image of fire fighters hoisting the American flag over the wreckage of the World Trade Center. In late May through early August, the U.S. Marine Drum and Bugle Corps and Silent Drill team perform at the Iwo Jima memorial every Tuesday evening at 7pm.

PAN AM FLIGHT 104 MEMORIAL CAIRN

A gift from Scotland to the people of the U.S., the Lockerbie Cairn memorializes the 270 lives lost in the terrorist attack on the United States when Pan Am flight 103 was bombed Dec. 21, 1988, over Lockerbie, Scotland . The 270 blocks of red Scottish sandstone come from Corsehill Quarry of Annan, Scotland, about eight miles southeast of Lockerbie and in the flight path of Flight 103. Corsehill Quarry, operating since 1820, has acquired a worldwide reputation for producing sandstone of superb quality. Stones from this quarry are used in many buildings in the United States including, most notably, the base stones of the Statue of Liberty.

SPACE SHUTTLE CHALLENGER

The Space Shuttle *Challenger* exploded on Jan. 28, 1986, just seconds after take off, killing all seven crewmembers. It was nearly two months before the remains were recovered from the ocean floor, about 18 miles off the shore of Cape Canaveral.

Capt. Michael Smith, the pilot of the *Challenger* was buried in Section 7A, Grave 208, May 3, 1986. On May 19, 1986, Francis "Dick" Scobee's cremated remains were interred in Section 46, Grave 1129. Early on the morning of May 20, 1986, the unidentified remains of all seven astronauts were buried near Scobee's grave in Section 46, now a memorial for all aboard that ill-fated space shuttle.

NURSES MEMORIAL

This memorial honors nurses who served in the U.S. armed forces in World War I, many of whom rest among the hundreds of nurses buried in Section 21 — also called the "Nurses Section." A granite statue of a nurse in uniform, sculpted by Frances Rich, and embraced by a sea of evergreens, presides over the memorial dedicated to the Army, Navy and Air Forces nurses who demonstrated heroism and valor during World War 1.

FREEDMAN'S VILLAGE

Near the Memorial Amphitheater is a plot of land the federal government dedicated as a model community for freed slaves on December 4, 1863. More than 1,100 freed slaves were given land, where they farmed and lived during and after the Civil War. They were forced to leave in 1890 when the estate was repurchased by the government and turned into a military installation. In Section 27, more than 3,800 former slaves, called "Contrabands" during the Civil War, are buried. Each of their headstones is marked with the word "Civilian" or "Citizen."

THE PENTAGON

Across the 14th Street Bridge from Washington, 703/695-1776, www.defenselink.mil.

Tours have been suspended. The best you can do is drive from Washington across the 14th Street Bridge to get a look at the uniquely shaped building. Ironically, Anthony and Barbara visited the Pentagon the week before the terrorist attack. They were too late for the tour – you must get there by 8am, in case the tours are renewed by the time you are reading this guide – but did receive a brochure discussing the Pentagon Metro Entrance Facility Project.

The project was established to provide more security for the Pentagon by moving the Metro facility from a few feet from the building to 280 feet away. This project is complete. The Pentagon also is in the construction phase of a memorial to September 11th victims.

Across the highway from the Pentagon is **Pentagon City**, a mall filled with shops and a wonderful Food Court.

MOUNT VERNON

703/780-2000, www.mountvernon.org, Open seven days a week, every day of the year, including holidays and Christmas, from April through August from 8am - 5pm and from March, September, October from 9am - 5pm and November through February from 9am - 4pm. Admission: Adults $9, children age 6-11 $4.50, under 6 free, seniors (with ID) $8.50. Gristmill Rates (when purchased with general admission): Adults $2, children (6-11)$1.50, children under 6 free, seniors (with ID) $2. If admission is only for Gristmill: Adults and seniors $4, children (6-11) $2, children under 6 free.

Getting There

By Car: From Washington, D.C, cross the Memorial Bridge, heading toward Arlington National Cemetery. While you are on the bridge, get in the center lane. At the circle on the Virginia side, go to the right, following the sign "George Washington Parkway" (do not head to "Arlington Cemetery"). Just after the circle, take the left-hand exit, marked "Parkway South/Alexandria/ Mount Vernon." Once on the Parkway, follow the signs to National Airport and continue south, through Alexandria. The parkway is renamed "Washington Street" in Alexandria. Mount Vernon is eight miles south of Alexandria, located at the large traffic circle at the end of Parkway.

By Metro: Take the yellow line to the Huntington stop. Board Fairfax Bus 101, which takes about 20 minutes to reach Mt. Vernon. Call 703/339-7200 for an up-to-date bus schedule.

By Tourbus: Both the Tourmobile (202/544-7950) and Grayline Tours (202/289-1995) have special, seasonal tours to Mt. Vernon. Call for current schedule and rates.

By Boat: Spirit Cruise Line, 202/554-8000, www.spiritcruises.com, offers a three-hour round-trip cruise aboard the Potomac Spirit to Mount Vernon from Washington, D.C. from March 16 through October 13, Tuesday through

Parent Tip

Looking for something to do bright and early? This is it! Most other museums and activities began at 10am, but Mt. Vernon swings open its doors at 8am April through August, 9am the rest of the year.

Sunday. The boat leaves from Pier 4, at 6th and Water Street SW, Washington, D.C., at 8:30am, arriving at Mount Vernon at 10am. It departs Mt. Vernon at 1:30pm, arriving at Pier 4 at 3pm. Round trip adult fare is $30.95, round-trip children's fare (6-11) is $20.95. Includes price of admission to Mt. Vernon.

Majestic Estate

One gains a deeper understanding of the man whom Washington was by meandering across his fields and gardens. The property ends by dropping down to the banks of the Potomac – a relaxing and peaceful vista. The perfect view to inspire revolutionary thought.

We decided against a group tour and instead rented the audio version. This gave us maximum flexibility to roam free and tarry where the mood fit. Well, the mood fit as soon as we passed through the gate. There, on the right, was a pen full of gently bleating sheep. "Bahhhh, Bahhhh," moaned the sheep. "Ohhhhh, Ohhhhhh," replied our little girl, as she just about propelled herself into the pen to hug those, cute, curly-haired sheep.

After mutual bahhing, we moved on. The road outside of the mansion is cobblestoned – the same cobblestone that Jefferson and Lafayette traversed to visit the honorable George. Very cool.

The mansion – so elegant and pristine — the white stone glistening in the sun. But wait a minute. Can it be? The house isn't made of stone; it's made of wood. Check out the Fun Fact below to find out how this is done.

Our children, surprisingly, enjoyed the house tour. Anthony took the tour again at age 12, and still enjoyed the walk through. Expect a line, but you are outdoors, so let the little ones explore while you wait.

Fun Fact: Don't you just love the look of white stone sparkling in the summer sun? Maybe you do, but that isn't what you're looking at here. Washington's mansion is an illusion of stone. Actually, it's just made out of wood. The process used to make it look like stone is called **rustication.** Long pine boards are grooved and beveled to create an appearance of masonry. Each board is varnished and painted. While the paint is still wet, fine sand is thrown on the wet paint. We all are still shaking our heads in disbelief!

The grounds are splendid, whether or not your children's interest is piqued by the historical significance of just about everything. Do go to the back of the house to where the land slopes to the wide Potomac River. This is a great photo opportunity. You can relax and enjoy the view and soft, summer breeze, while the kids roll, jump and scamper before you're off to another traveling adventure. No food or drink allowed and it is enforced! But, there is a food court adjacent to the home.

Our children also enjoyed the upper garden, established like a little maze. It reminded them of Beatrix Potter's garden and off they went searching for that mischievous Peter Rabbit.

Fun Fact: Every U.S. Navy ship that passes Mt. Vernon pays tribute to America's first president by lowering its flag to half-mast, officers and crew salute and the ship's bell tolls. This tradition has been going on continuously since 1801!

Walk through the grounds to see the barn, carriage house, kitchen and smokehouse. During Washington's stay at Mt. Vernon, his property covered more than 8,000 acres operated by hundreds of workers. A virtual self-contained city!

If you enjoy walking down and up a steep slope, wander down to the pioneer farm. Here, you are right on the waterfront and can watch farm life as it occurred in the 1700s. No Paris Hilton here. Guides dressed in period attire can answer all of your questions. And, you will learn of some of the inventive ways Mr. Washington and his staff got all the hard work done.

The museum at Mt. Vernon is small, but quite intriguing. Of most interest to everyone is the display of George Washington's false teeth!

Fun Fact: Outside of the White House, Mt. Vernon is the most visited historic home in America. Mr. Washington should be proud. He designed it himself.

Mt. Vernon offers several special tours and events, some designed specifically with children in mind:

George Washington: Pioneer Farmer site and 16-sided Treading Barn, south of the mansion, down many wide steps, on the waterfront, April 1 through October 31. Down on the farm, that's what this event is all about. Step into the shoes of a farmer and hoe, feed animals and, well, do the things a farmer does. Great fun for all of us city slickers. The four-acre site features rare-breed barn animals – oxen, mules, roosters, sheep, chickens. Seasonal activities guide visitors through 18th-century farming techniques, including watching the horses and mules treading for wheat. The eight fields remind us that Washington was first and foremost a farmer. Get a glimpse of Washington's advanced farming practices and crop rotation scheme. **Wagon rides** in April are a fun diversion. They operate Friday, Saturday and Sunday from 10am to 2pm. This site is just a five-minute walk south of the Mansion, down (and then up) a flight of wide steps, adjacent to the Wharf on the Potomac River. The site is open year-round with hands-on activities from April through October.

Slave Life at Mt. Vernon Tour, offered daily April 1 through October 31 at 10am, noon, 2pm and 4pm. Years ago upon visiting Thomas Jefferson's home in Monticello, we noticed a sign over a backroom indicating "Servant's Quarters." As far as we know, servants get paid. After so many years, the fact that even the nation's most admired men had slaves has come to light. So here it is, a slave-life tour of Mt. Vernon. The 30-minute guided walking tour introduces visitors to the daily lives of the Mount Vernon slaves. See where these men, women and children lived and worked, learn about their families, and gain an understanding of their legacy at Mount Vernon.

Gardens and Landscape Tour, offered daily April 1 through October 31 at 11am, 1pm and 3pm. Stroll through the grounds and gardens that Washington designed and nurtured. See some of the original trees that have stood guard through the centuries. This is a 30-minute walking tour. April 20, through May 5 are Gardening Days at Mt. Vernon. Make a purchase at the annual Plant, Gift and Garden sale.

Mt. Vernon Wine Festival, mid-May, tickets on sale mid-March, from 6pm to 9pm. Sample some of Virginia's best wine and learn about the history of winemaking under the stars at Mt. Vernon. Enjoy jazz music while you watch 18th-century craft demonstrations (brings new meaning to multi-cultural!) Even tour Washington's hidden wine cellars. We have our tickets and will report back in this book's update on the appropriateness of this event for families with children.

Time to Eat

Eating and drinking are not permitted once you enter the gate, however, there is a full-service Food Court Pavilion (703/799-8688) and a delightful restaurant located just outside the gate for hungry travelers. From gourmet burgers and heavenly french fries to Mrs. Fields cookies and cool hand-dipped ice cream treats, the Food Court Pavilion has something for you. Enjoy your snacks inside the airy Pavilion, or munch your lunch at the outside terrace.

The Mount Vernon Inn serves lunch (11am to 3:30pm) every day except Christmas and dinner (Monday through Saturday 5pm to 9pm) every day. Dinner is elegant, candle-lit, serving colonial and regional cuisine. Waiters don period attire. It is a grand ending to a charming afternoon at Mt. Vernon.

Time to Shop

For some reason, this shop reminds us of *Babes in Toyland*. Old, colonial-time toys still hold magic for our 21st-century children. The children's section is expansive. George and Martha bears, wooden swords and guns, leather pouch with marbles, delightful rag dolls, wooden-maple fifes, the Game of Graces (where opponents send gaily beribboned hoops swirling toward each other to be caught on the tips of slender wands). The big hit was the 18th-century milled dollar toy whizzer (round disk with two center holes through which a string was passed, when twisted and then pulled straight the string sends the disk swirling, making an incredible whizzing noise, hence the name). Who needs gameboys?

By 2006, expect high-tech to come to the farm. The good Mt. Vernon folks are working to make Washington's home more interactive. Families also will be able to enjoy a Steven Spielberg short film on America's first president.

OLD TOWN ALEXANDRIA

Located 6 miles south of Washington, D.C., across the Potomac River.

Note that the road to Old Town (Route 1) is the same road that takes you to Mt. Vernon. You could spend the morning/early afternoon in Mt. Vernon and end up for a wonderful evening in Old Town.

Getting There

By Car: To access the city from I-95, take the Route 1 exit north (Patrick Street). Turn right on King Street to reach downtown Alexandria. From National Airport, take the George Washington Memorial Parkway south, it becomes Washington Street which passes through downtown. From Washington, D.C., take I-395 south to Route 1 south. After passing through Crystal City and Potomac Yards, Route 1 becomes Henry Street. Downtown is left on King Street.

By Metro: Take the yellow or blue line to King Street.

Historic Old Town

In many ways a time capsule of colonial America. If you can't get make the drive to Williamsburg, this may be the next best thing. Much of present-day Alexandria was included in a 6,000-acre land grant from Sir William Berkeley, Governor of Virginia, awarded to Robert Howsing, an English ship captain, in October 1669. Howsing's reward was decreed by King Charles II for Howsing's courage in bringing about 120 people to live in Virginia.

Fun Fact: Howsing is not a good role model for anti-tobacco. Can you believe he sold his 6,000-acre land grant for 6,000 pounds of tobacco to John Alexander? All Howsing's dreams to be remembered in perpetuity went up in smoke. The land now bears Alexander's name.

Alexandria was incorporated in 1779 and became a port of entry for foreign vessels and a major export town for flour and hemp. George Washington maintained a town house here and served as a Trustee of Alexandria (his home at Mt. Vernon is just a few miles away).

The city knew war. During the Revolutionary War, George Washington drilled militia troops at Market Square and the town served as a supply and hospital center. Robert E. Lee grew up in Alexandria. His father, "Light Horse Harry" Lee, was a Revolutionary War general.

During the Civil War, Alexandria immediately was occupied by Union forces (May 1861) and became a logistical supply center for the federal army. During this era, several forts were constructed to defend the city of Washington. **Fort Ward Park** contains one of these restored forts.

The **Torpedo Factory** was built during World War I and again used in World War II as a United States munitions factory. Today it is an award-winning example of adaptive reuse and shines as home to shops, restaurants, residences and offices on the vibrant waterfront of Alexandria.

Strict architectural and demolition control has saved many of Alexandria's historic sites.

Alexandria is full of history, politics and parks. Detect a sense of restlessness? A family Civil War brewing? Take your children to Waterfront Park and let them run with the wind, feed pigeons and board the 125-foot schooner, *Alexandria* (open Saturday and Sunday from noon to 5pm, free admission).

FORT WARD PARK AND MUSEUM

4301 West Braddock Road, 703/838-4848, **Metro Stop:** King Street (yellow line, then take DASH bus #5), Park open daily 9am to sunset; museum Tuesday through Saturday 9am to noon and Sunday noon-5pm.

The Civil War comes alive at Fort Ward Park, a short drive from Old Town. This 45-acre park hosts six mounted guns, a fort and a reproduction of an officer's hut. Lots of room to run, gallop and re-enact the Civil War (oh, actually that's just sibling warfare going on!) The museum houses sundry Civil War weapons and other exhibits that demonstrate the every-day life of citizens during the Civil War (1861-1865).

BLACK HISTORY RESOURCE CENTER

638 N. Alfred Street (Entrance on Wythe Street), 703/838-4356, **Metro Stop:** Braddock Road (blue or yellow line – walk across the parking lot and bear right to the corner of West and Wythe streets, Follow Wythe Street five blocks east. The Center is at the corner of Whyteh and Alfred), open Tuesday through Saturday 10am to 4pm; Sunday 1pm to 5pm; Closed Mondays, New Year's Day, Easter, Thanksgiving, Christmas.

Five African-American men in 1939 staged a sit-down strike in the city's segregated Queen Street Library. Although the men were arrested for their act of civil disobedience, the town built the Robert Robinson Library in 1940. This segregated library for African-Americans was used until the city was desegregated in the early 1960s. The library now forms an integral part of the Alexandria Black History Resource Center.

Besides the library, the center's museum offers a collection of paintings, photographs, books and other memorabilia that document the African-American experience in Alexandria and Virginia from 1749 to the present. The Center also presents a special collection on the history and graduates of the Parker-Gray School.

TORPEDO FACTORY

105 North Union Street, 703/838-4565, www.torpedofaactory.org, Open daily 10am to 5pm; Closed New Year's Day, Easter, Fourth of July, Thanksgiving and Christmas.

The Torpedo Factory has been converted to a fantastic arts center –from pottery to sculpture, from painting to photography. Visit 84 working studios, 8 group studios and 6 galleries. On the third floor is the **Alexandria Archeology Museum**, where you can visit a working archeological lab and inspect artifacts found in Alexandria.

The second Thursday of each month is **Art Night** (6pm to 9pm). Enjoy a leisurely stroll through the cobblestone streets of Alexandria and end your evening at the Torpedo Factory to see what the artists have in store for you. Children welcome.

ROBERT E. LEE HOME

607 Oronoco Street, 703/548-8454, Open Monday through Saturday 10am to 4pm and Sunday 1pm to 4pm, Closed Easter and Thanksgiving and from December 15 through January 31. Tours: Docent-led tours are on going throughout the day.

This stately, Federal townhouse was home to Robert E. Lee when he was a young lad. George and Martha Washington were frequent visitors here, as was the Marquis de Lafayette. Authentic period furniture is on display throughout the house. Our children enjoyed the nursery, where homemade toys and Native American arrowheads are on view. This area once was a Native American hunting ground.

THE LYCEUM: ALEXANDRIA'S HISTORY MUSEUM

201 S. Washington Street, 703/838-4994, **Metro Stop:** King Street (yellow or blue line, Cross the parking lot and turn left, one half block to Prince Street. Turn left (east) on Prince Street and walk about one mile to Washington Street. Turn right, and the Lyceum will be on your right. Or take the Dash Bus to King and Washington Streets, turn right and walk one block past Prince Street. Call (703) 370-DASH for bus schedules and information, or check the schedules posted at the station), Open Monday to Saturday from 10am to 5pm, Sunday from 1pm to 5pm, Closed New Year's Day, Thanksgiving, Christmas Eve, Christmas.

Alexandria's history museum has quite a history. It began in 1839 when a group of gentlemen, calling themselves The Alexandria Lyceum, decided they needed a place to read quietly, engage in scientific exploration and attend lectures. Since then, it became a Civil War hospital, private home, office building, the nation's first Bicentennial Center and now, whew, a museum. Learn all about the rich history not only of this building, but of Alexandria.

GREAT FALLS, VIRGINA

GREAT FALLS PARK

9200 Old Dominion Drive, 703/285-2965.

Dramatic falls, cascading water thundering past boulders, rocks and sand. This is Great Falls, a beautiful rendering of the strength and majesty of the natural world. Geologically unique, the Falls began to emerge during the last ice age when the ocean levels dropped forcing the Potomac River to carve a deeper path to the sea. The top-level of rock was overrun, exposing a much harder rock formation called the Piedmont. This hard layer is comprised of metamorphic and igneous rock (for all you students of rocks and minerals). Fault areas of loosening rock have been plowed through ensuing years by the force of the Potomac River, changing the river's course and creating the incredible spectacle you now see.

Parent Tip

The Falls are gorgeous, but also treacherous. Stay on the paths and the observation decks to view the falls. Every year tragedy strikes, so be careful.

∽

The overlooks to the Falls date to the early 1900s. At that time, D.C. denizens traveled by train to the Falls, which was home to an amusement park. Now, nature amuses visitors. At the Falls, you can hike 15 miles of trails), bike, birdwatch, white water raft and horseback ride. Contact the Great Falls Park for more information (703/285-2965).

Our children and their friend Kathleen enjoyed the Nature Center children's room, complete with Native American artifacts and Checkers, a corn snake. The short slide-show presentation provided an enjoyable overview of Great Falls. But, they really were excited by the Park Ranger's tour of the Falls. Geology was the lesson of the day. So if your children are into fossils, rocks and dirt, this is the tour for you. We found the girls sharpening sticks, while Anthony meandered over to watch an artist paint the golden sun delicately dabbing the sharp rocks and flowing water.

Time to Eat
A concession stand provides uninteresting but palatable food. Bring your own, if you can, there are many picnic tables dotting the Park's grassy floor.

Time to Shop
Adjacent to the Children's Room is a tiny gift shop, overflowing with fun gifts for kids. Lots of great nature books and cute cuddlies.

NEARBY MARYLAND

GLEN ECHO PARK
MacArthur Boulevard at Goldboro Road.

Getting There
By Car: From Washington, D.C., take Massachusetts Avenue toward Wisconsin Avenue, continue until Massachusetts Avenue ends. Make a left on Goldsboro Road and continue to MacArthur Boulevard. Turn right for one, short, block and turn left into the parking lot.
By Metro/Bus: Take the red line to Friendship Heights or Bethesda stops. Take Montgomery County (Maryland) Ride-On Bus #29. For more information on schedules and fares, call 240/777-7433.

Things to Do
Glen Echo Park was born in 1881 as a place to teach the sciences, arts, languages and literature to the masses. By 1900 it was on its way to become a premier amusement park for the Washington area. Bumper cars and a splendid **Dentzel Carousal** dominated the frontier. But in 1968, the Glen Echo Amusement Park sadly ran its last ride, shrugged its shoulders and shriveled into disrepair.

In full circle, Glen Echo Park is fast becoming the cultural arts center its originators dreamed of. The Carousal is a draw for all local children. Art and dancing classes dominate. And, children's theater is a boon to the contemporary success of the park.

The **Dentzel Carousal** is a star attraction at Glen Echo. Artistically carved and painted, the menagerie spins gracefully round the indoor carousal. Find the horses, rabbits (a favorite of Carravita's), tigers, giraffes, ostriches and cats. Can you spot the lead horse? (It's the largest one in the outside circle). These well-cared for animals were saved from extinction in 1970 by a group of local citizens. Typically, historic carousals were dismantled, with collectors purchasing individual animals for their personal use. The Carousal runs from May 3 to October 1 on weekends from 11:30am to 6pm and Wednesday and Thursday from 10am to 2pm.

Fun Facts:
 • Who was Dentzel? Gustav Dentzel, son of a carousal maker in Germany, moved to America in 1860 to make his mark in the carousal business. He began his business in Philadelphia, which remained all in the family until 1929.
 • More than one thousand lights beam from the carousal, reflecting off the inner mirrors and making for a gay ride round and round.

Adventure Theater is the Washington area's longest-running children's theater. Located in the old Arcade Building, Adventure Theater performances are for the young and young at heart. Imaginative productions of past and modern-day fairy tales and fables delight children and their adult companions.

Carol Leahy, artistic director of Adventure Theater, is not only an amazing theatrical professional but operates from a love of children. She masterfully and magically has directed our children's school play for the past four years. From The Mikado to Peter Pan, Carol has helped give many children their first taste of live theater – including our Anthony who was thrilled to play Captain Hook. "Split me infinitives," but we think Adventure Theater and Ms. Leahy are the "sun and the moon and the stars," to quote both Captain Hook and his Neverland nemesis, Tiger Lily. Enjoy an afternoon performance here or at the fun Puppet Company Playhouse.

For more information on Adventure Theater call, 301/320-5331, www.nps.gov/glec/adtheat, Performances Saturday and Sunday at 1:30pm and 3:30pm, Tickets are $5 for adults and children.

Rod puppets, hand puppets, marionettes. They're all here. **The Puppet Company Playhouse** is the only East Coast theater between New York City and Atlanta that is dedicated entirely to puppetry. For more information call 301/320-6668, www.nps.gov/glec/gepuppet. Performances Wednesday, Thursday and Friday at 10am and 11:30am and Saturday and Sunday at 11:30am and 1pm., Tickets are $5 for children and adults.

On the grounds of Glen Echo is a delightful little playground for children waiting for a performance to begin, or for releasing energy before being strapped into the car!

Directly across the parking lot is the historic home of **Clara Barton,** 5801 Oxford Road, 301/492-6245, www.nps.gov/clba, Open daily 10am to 5pm, Closed New Year's Day, Thanksgiving and Christmas, Tours: You must take the tour to see the home. They begin every hour on the hour, the first one at 10am, the last at 4pm.

Clara Barton, heroine extraordinaire. Perhaps one of the first women to work out of her home, Clara Barton lived in this house, ran the American Red Cross from here and also used the building as a warehouse for disaster relief supplies. She moved in with 30 wagonloads of belongings in 1897 and resided here until her death in 1912 at the age of 90. The uniqueness of the building, and of the woman, makes this home an interesting and insightful tour for children.

GREAT FALLS PARK, MARYLAND

Potomac, Maryland. C & O Canal and McCarther Boulevard, 301/413-0720 .

Yes, Great Falls also can be enjoyed on the Maryland side of the Potomac, though it is not as popular as the Virginia side. Look for the **Billy-Goat Trail,** a fun adventure for many children. However, be aware that while the trail starts out relatively flat and easy, it quickly becomes steep and rocky. It is a two-mile hike for children and adults adept at climbing rocky paths. The views as you perch between rocks – out-of-this-world! The Falls are thunderous, with white water cascading down steep falls. We always enjoy watching the kayakers who skillfully navigate the treacherous waters.

Oh yes, if you've made it through the two miles of Billy Goat Trail and are not looking forward to marching back through the rocks, you can simply walk back to the starting point on the very flat, no big rocks towpath.

Chapter 8

FIELD TRIPS

BALTIMORE

Tourist Information

Baltimore Area Visitors Center, 451 Light Street, Baltimore, Maryland, 21202, 410/837-4636 or 800/282-6632, www.baltimore.org, a branch office is located on the west side of the Inner Harbor.

Getting There

By car: Baltimore, Maryland, is about 40 miles northeast of downtown Washington, D.C. By car, take Route I-95. Get off at Exit 53 and continue on I-395 North to Oriole Park (Camden Yard). Turn right on Pratt Street, which runs parallel to the Inner Harbor. Find parking! There are numerous lots and garages in the vicinity.

By train: A fun way to travel to Baltimore is by Amtrak. Trains leave frequently between Washington's Union Station and Baltimore's Penn Station. Plan on the train taking a little over one-half hour. You have several options for trains:

Metroliner: (most expensive) Metroliner service roundtrip from Washington to Baltimore runs $228 for travel during the week and $198 over the weekend. It is an express train with reserved seating.

Conventional Train: (business and unreserved coach class) The conventional train costs $150 round trip. It is more expensive on Friday and Sunday after 11am. There is only a 10-minute time difference between the conventional train and the Metroliner. The only reason to spend so much more money is to reserve a seat. Because the train schedule is so frequent for both trains, we recommend you save the cash and go conventional.

I'm Hungry
McCormick & Schmick's $$-$$$, Pier 5 at Inner Harbor, 410/234-1300.

Sit at the outdoor patio and devour the views of the Chesapeake Bay and Baltimore's skyline. We nod in agreement with Baltimore Magazine's rating of McCormick & Schmick's as the "Best View Restaurant." Try the Maryland lump crab cakes or go the full monty with lobster from Maine. Michael recommends the oysters on a half-shell. And, there's a kids' menu featuring fish and chips, chicken cheeseburger, pizza, spaghetti and grilled cheese – for $3.95 each. Top it off with an ice-cream sundae. Service was lovely. We're coming back.

Food Court $, Light Street Pavilion, Harborplace

Whoa, Italian funnel cake, humus, ice-cream, the best french fries and seafood delicacies, you can find almost anything your children crave at this food court.

Phillips $$, Light Street Pavilion, Harborplace, 410/685-6600

Yummy seafood dishes, live music and a waterside patio. It is especially wonderful at night, with stars shining and lights glistening off the water. Very popular, long lines.

Planet Hollywood $-$$, Pratt Street Pavilion, Harborplace, 410/685-7827.

Typical Planet Hollywood fare – hamburgers to salads – and atmosphere –Hollywood glitter and glitz.

Hard Rock Café $, Power Plant, 601 East Pratt Street, 410/347-7625.

The music's loud, the food's okay. Teens will love it and you'll walk down memory lane.

Where Are We Going Now?
INNER HARBOR
Urban renewal takes on new meaning in good, ole' "Bawlamer." If you knew Baltimore they way we knew Baltimore pre-Inner Harbor days, you would think us nuts to recommend the city as a field trip from Washington. Barbara remembers coming here when they started to construct Inner Harbor. From high on the hill of Ft. McHenry, she could see the industrial sea harbor, the construction site and, well, not much else.

Now the ugly duckling has matured into a most beautiful swan. A state-of-the-art aquarium, fascinating science center, paddleboats, water taxis, fabulous restaurants and nightlife galore! This is the new Baltimore, begging for you to not only enjoy Harborplace, but to see even more of Baltimore's bounty beyond the harbor.

The city is one of America's oldest. Established in 1729, it was named after the founder of Maryland, George Calvert, the first Lord Baltimore. For a short time during the Revolutionary War, it served as the nascent nation's capital. A tough town, it defended itself against British attack in 1812.

It wasn't until after World War II that the little city that could broke down. Similar to other large urban cities in America, as went the manufacturing industry, so went Baltimore. And that was down the tubes. It took the ingenuity and inspiration of local citizens and a highly active and activist mayor to turn the city around. Lucky for you, Baltimore's true star-spangled colors are soaring.

NATIONAL AQUARIUM

Pier 3, 501 East Pratt Street, 410/576-3800, www.aqua.org, Open July and August 9am to 8pm daily; November through February, Saturday through Thursday from 10am to 5pm and Friday 10am to 8pm; March-June, September-October, Saturday through Thursday from 9am to 5pm and Friday from 9am to 8pm, Admission: adults $14, seniors, $10.50, children 3-11 $7.50, and children under 3 are free. Reserved advance tickets can be purchased through TicketMaster at 410/481-SEAT, or 800/551-SEAT.

WOW! What an aquarium. Outside of Monterey, California, we vote this the top aquarium we've ever visited. The architecture alone – glass triangles and neon waves at the water's edge – entices you to discover the mysteries of what lies inside. Let's see, which exhibit did our kids like more? The 260,000-gallon tank that contains six different species of rays as well as small nurse, sandbar and bonnethead sharks? Mesmerizing. How about the new exhibit featuring hundreds of seahorses? Magical. Or the electric eel, which could produce 600 volts to capture, and deep-fry, food? Marvelous.

Do take in the dolphin show. More than leaps and somersaults, visitors learn about the adaptive strategies dolphins use in their ocean environment at this multi-media presentation. Did you know every dolphin has its own signature whistle?

Also, check out the Children's Discovery Cove, where you can hold marine animals – a horseshoe crab or a sea star. Informative guides patiently answer each child's question.

Fun Fact: Rays, sharks and skates are members of the same class of animals. They all have cartilage instead of a bony skeleton.

Time to Eat

The Pavilion Café on the ground level has Pizza Hut and Breyer's ice cream. It's not bad, but why stop here when the entire Inner Harbor lies before you?

Time to Shop

Carravita loves dolphins, and this shop is the dolphin channel. Of course, many other items are carried, but we only got to see the dolphin section. Look for T-shirts, games, toys, educational videos, books and much more.

BALTIMORE MARITIME MUSEUM

Pier 3, E. Pratt Street (to purchase tickets), 410/396-3854, Open Sunday through Thursday from 10am to 5:30pm and Friday and Saturday from 10am to 6:30pm, (hours change during winter months: Open Friday through Sunday only 10:30am to 5pm), Admission: adults, $6.00, seniors $5.00, children 6-14 $3, under 5 free and active duty military with ID $2.

Ships and submarines. Walk up the plank and tour the ships of the Baltimore Maritime Museum: The Coast Guard Cutter Tanney, the Lightship Chesapeake, and the World War II submarine the U.S.S. TORSK. The sub is a particular hit with children. Those long, narrow passageways, tiny sleeping quarters, and massive torpedoes. The sub once had an active life both during WW II and in the naval blockade of Cuba.

The Tanney, a retired Coast Guard cutter, survived Pearl Harbor. And, the Chesapeake is a floating lighthouse built in 1930.

Want to know more about U.S. naval history? Or, simply want a great view of the water? Stroll over to the Seven-Foot Knoll Lighthouse. Built in 1856, this is the oldest "screwpile" lighthouse in Maryland. Initially, it stood guard at the mouth of the Patapsco River, where it marked the shoal known as the Seven-Foot Knoll for 133 years.

A small exhibit and even smaller gift shop can be found inside the Lighthouse.

U.S.S. CONSTELLATION

Pier 1, 301 East Pratt Street, 410/539-1797, www.constellation.org, Open May 1 to October 14 daily from 10am to 6pm and from October 15 to April 30 from 10am to 4pm. Hours may be extended in the summer months, Closed Thanksgiving and Christmas, Admission: adults $6.50, seniors $5, children 6 to 14 $3.50 and children under 6 are free.

Another awesome ship to tour. The U.S.S. Constellation was launched in August 1864. From 1859-1861 it engaged in an anti-slavery patrol, capturing three slave ships. It also served in the Civil War, protecting U.S. merchant ships in the Mediterranean Sea from Confederate raiders. It is the last all-sail warship built by the U.S. Navy. Surveying the waters, Anthony thrilled us with a few lines from Captain Hook: "How still the night is . . . " (for all you Peter Pan lovers!)

Call about special tours. One in particular is quite a lot of fun for children 10 and older. The Powder Monkey Tour calls on all children 10 and up to learn about the young boys who served as powder monkeys on this ship. In a hands-on tour, children will learn how boys from 11 to 18 lived and worked in Mr. Lincoln's Navy. Kids get to don era attire and even hoist up the anchor. Call 410/539-1797, then press 3 for up-to-date schedule information.

MARYLAND SCIENCE CENTER

601 Light Street, 410/685-5225, www.mdsci.org, Open Monday through Friday from 10am to 5pm, Saturday 10am to 6pm and Sunday from noon to 6pm, The IMAX theater is open after hours and the Crosby Ramsey Memorial Observatory is open after hours on Thursday, Admission: adults $8, children 3-12 $6, seniors $7, IMAX tickets are $7 for all, special feature IMAX rates are higher. There are packages for visiting the museum and seeing the IMAX.

Better than an amusement park. Life here is hands-on. And the science – everywhere. Just try to get your children out of the Science Arcade. So many bells, whistles, magnets, mechanics, sights and sounds. Once you've pulled them out of that room, check out Outer Space Place. Your family will be lost in space here. Outer Space Place is home to the Hubble Space Telescope National Visitor Center, so you'll get lots of up-to-date info on Hubble discoveries.

Other exhibits feature the Chesapeake, Dino Digs, and a Demonstration Stage, where all kinds of wild and wacky science shows occur. Don't forget to check out the Observatory. Stargazing Thursdays are fascinating. Do remember: The Observatory is outside on the roof. Dress appropriately and call 410/545-2999 after 5pm to ensure the Observatory will be open that evening.

FORT McHENRY NATIONAL MONUMENT

End of East Fort Avenue, 410/962-4290, www.nps.gov/fomc, Grounds open daily from June 1 to September 2 from 8am to 8pm; Fort and Visitor Center from 8am to 7:45pm, Park closed Christmas and New Year's Day; rest of the year, grounds open from 8am to 5pm; Fort and Visitor Center, daily 8am to 4:45pm., Admission $5, seniors and children under 17 are free.

Imagine watching the cannons boom, with gunfire flares lighting up the sky . . . and the American Stars and Stripes. From the vantagepoint of Fort McHenry, guardian of Baltimore's harbor, Francis Scott Key immortalized America's battle against the British on September 13-14, 1814, by penning a song that captured the spirit of the nascent nation. The Star-Spangled Banner continues to musically represent America from classrooms to the Olympics.

Plan your visit around the **flag-change ceremony**, held daily 9:30am and 7:30pm (summer months), 9:30am to 4:30pm the rest of the year, weather permitting.

Make your first stop the Fort McHenry **Visitor's Center** (open from June 2 to September 3 from 8am to 7:45pm, rest of the year from 8am to 4:45pm).

Enjoy the exhibits noting the Fort's history and the film, The Defense of Fort McHenry.

The **Star Fort Museum** is just steps away from the Visitor Center (410/962-4290, open June 2 to September 3 from 8am to 7:45pm and the rest of the year from 8am to 4:45pm. Stop here to see an electric battle map, restored flagpole and commander's quarters, guard house, powder magazine and the enlisted men's quarters.

BABE RUTH BIRTHPLACE AND BALTIMORE ORIOLES MUSEUM

216 Emory Street, 410/727-1539, www.baberuthmuseum.com, Open daily April through October from 10am to 5pm; November through March 10am to 4pm, remains open until 7pm when Orioles are playing in Baltimore, Admission: Adults $6, seniors $4, children 5 to 16 $3, children under 5 are free.

Take me out to . . . Babe Ruth's birthplace. Home of the slugger. This is all things Babe – from a student-produced calendar he made and baseball mitt from Babe's school days at St. Mary's School to his Louisville Slugger bat used in 1927 when Ruth hit 60 home runs.

The museum also features Oriole baseball memorabilia.

BALLPARK TOURS

Oriole Park at Camden Yards, 410/547-6234, www.TheOreioles.com, Open April through September Monday-Friday at 11am, noon, 1pm and 2pm; Saturday at 10:30am, 11am, 11:30am, noon, 12:30pm, 1pm, 1:30pm and 2pm; Sunday at 12:30pm, 1pm, 2pm and 3pm, Admission: Adults $5, children 12 and under $4 and seniors 55 and over, $4.

Baseball fanatics will love this ballpark tour. Come see the Orioles' dugout, club level suites and more on this 1-hour tour.

ANNAPOLIS

Tourist Information

Annapolis and Anne Arundel County Conference and Visitors Center, 29 West Street, Annapolis, Maryland, 21401, 410/280-0445, www.visit-annapolis.org. A kiosk is open on the City Dock from April through October, daily 10am to 5pm.

Getting There

By car: 30 miles east of Washington, D.C. Take Route U.S. 50 to exit 24. This is Rowe Boulevard, or Maryland-70. Head southeast straight into Annapolis. We usually drive right into the historic center and use a parking garage. However, you also can park at the Navy-Marine Corps Stadium and take a shuttle bus into town. The shuttle runs every 20 minutes on weekdays only, from 6:30am to 8pm.

By bus: Greyhound/Trailways offers limited bus service between Washington and Annapolis. Call 800/231-2222.

I'm Hungry

Treaty of Paris $$$, Maryland Inn, 16 Church Circle, near the State House, 410/216-6340.

A charming 18th-century inn that serves classic continental cuisine. You also can find plain, old, modern American cooking, too. This is a bit elegant, so take a good look at your kids – squabbling and shabby or harmonious and put-together (for at least during the period you plan to eat!). Then decide.

Middleton Tavern $$, 2 Market Space, 410/263-3323

Great choice for families. On the waterfront, outdoor service. Known for its seafood, but also serves hamburgers and other kid favorites.

Where Are We Going Now?
U.S. NAVAL ACADEMY

Visitor's Center located on King George Street, inside Gate 1, 410/263-6933, the Center is open from March through December from 9am to 5pm and from 9am to 4pm January and February, Closed New Year's Day, Thanksgiving and Christmas; Visiting Hours: 9am to 5pm, or sunset, whichever is later. Enter through Gate 1 at the corner of Randall Street and King George Street, Tours: Guided walking tours of the grounds leave from the Center and are offered Monday through Saturday from 9:30am to 3pm , Sunday from 12:30pm to 3pm, every half hour, Admission: $6, preschoolers free.

Established in an old army fort in 1845, the U.S. Naval Academy has grown to become an illustrious school situated at the mouth of the Severn River. Many historic sites are featured on this 238-acre campus, including:

Take a whiff of the sea air. Listen to the seagulls sing. The **City Dock** is the heart of historic Annapolis. Turn your back to the sea, and the skyline you view is not much different from that seen by folks in the 18th century.

From here, tour boats, water taxis, workboats and pleasure craft dock. During the summer, enjoy Navy Band concerts on the Dock. In the fall, the largest boat shows in the world are held at the Annapolis City Dock.

Most impressive, at the foot of the dock is the Kunta Kinte plaque, commemorating the site where the young Kunta Kinte, from the Roots (Alex Haley) novel, was sold into slavery.

The **Naval Academy Museum**, packed with academy lore, exquisite model ships and mementos of American naval history. Located in Preble Hall on

Maryland Avenue, the museum is open from 9am to 5pm Monday through Saturday and 11am to 5pm on Sunday. Call 410/293-2108 for more information.

The brigade holds a **lunchtime formation** about 12:10pm on weekdays, weather permitting, in Tecumeseh Court, in front of Bancroft Hall. Visitors also may watch the brigade's **formal dress parades** on Worden Field, held at various times during the spring, summer and fall. Call 410/293-2108 for schedule.

Navy Chapel is the architectural centerpiece of The Yard. The United States' first naval hero, John Paul Jones (of "I have not yet begun to fight" fame), is buried in a vault beneath the sanctuary.

Athletic Events are open to the public. Call the Naval Academy Athletic Association at 410/268-6060 for more information.

BANNEKER-DOUGLASS MUSEUM

84 Franklin Street, 410/216-6180, www.marylandhistoricaltrust.net/bdm.html, open Tuesday through Friday from 10am-3pm and Saturday 12pm-4pm.

The former church, built by free blacks in 1874, is named after Benjamin Banneker, the Maryland-born mathematician who helped to survey and lay out the District of Columbia and Frederick Douglass, an escaped slave who led the abolition movement and was a Renaissance man. The exhibits include on slave and religious artifacts.

WILLIAM PACA HOUSE

186 Prince George Street, 410/267-7619.

Quite an elegant landmark. Paca was a wealthy young planter who a signer of the Declaration of Independence. Stop in at the splendid garden, two-acres, five terraces, a wilderness garden and the kids will love the fish-shaped pond.

THE STATE HOUSE

State Circle.

Actually, this is the third state house for Maryland. The first burned down in 1704. The second was razed in 1769 because it was too small to house the burgeoning state government. Joseph Clark, an Annapolis architect and builder, designed and built the State House you see today around 1788.

Fun Fact: Joseph Clark, architect of the State House, used Benjamin Franklin's notion of lightening rods in his original design. It may have been a political statement favoring Franklin's theories of protecting public buildings from lightening – theories that were opposed by King George III.

MARYLAND GOVERNMENT HOUSE

State Circle, 410/974-3531.

The house has been home to Maryland governors for over 125 years. This Georgian-style home was built in. Call for information on reserving a tour of the house.

ANNAPOLIS SUMMER GARDEN THEATER

143 Compromise Street, 410/268-9212, www.summergarden.com.

Fun summer theater – from Shakespeare to the best of Broadway – under the stars and located close to the Dock.

COLONIAL WILLIAMSBURG

Tourist Information

Colonial Williamsburg Foundation, P.O. Box 1776, Williamsburg, Virginia 23187, 757/220-7645 or 800/HISTORY, www.colonialwilliamsburg.org, or www.history.org. For information about tours and tickets, call 757/220-7645. Another option for information and reservations is the Williamsburg Convention and Visitors Bureau at 800/368-6511.

At the Visitors' Center on the edge of the historic site, you will be able to purchase several passes that will allow entry into the buildings. Strolling through the streets is free. The **Patriot's Pass** (adults $34, children 6-12 $19.50) admits you to everything, including shopping and entertainment discounts, valid for one year. The **Colonist's Pass** (adults $30, children 6-12 $17) admits you to almost all of the area's buildings and shops and two of the three museums. It is good for two consecutive days. Then, there is the **Basic Pass** (Adults $26, children 6-12 $15), which lets you see the orientation film and admits you to most of the area's buildings.

Make sure you stop at the Visitor's Center to get a map of the sites, information on restaurants and general lay of the land.

Getting There

By car: Williamsburg is about 150 miles southeast of Washington. From downtown Washington, D.C., take I-95 South to I-295 South, then I-64 East. From I-64 take Exit 238 (Williamsburg/Camp Peary) and follow the signs to the Visitors' Center. Or, for a more scenic route, pass up I-64 and instead exit off I-295 to follow the lovely U.S. 60 East. Parking is free. Then, take a bus from there to the edge of the Historic District.

By train: Trains run regularly between Washington, D.C., and Williamsburg. However, the schedule allows hardly enough time to turn this into a day trip. We've added some hotel information for those wishing to spend a night.

Which One is My Room?

For information on packages, of which there are many, call 800/447-8679, or contact the Williamsburg Hotel/Motel Association at 800/447-8679.

Several key points to consider: Williamsburg is a small town that welcomes well over 4 million tourists a year. Hotels, motels and B&Bs book up fast. So do call ahead. Also, Williamsburg is the land of hotel-package deals. Golf, kids, history, whatever your interest, there's a deal for you. Check the official Colonial Williamsburg site www.Williamsburg.com and click on hotels to find packages.

Courtyard by Marriott, just east of town, 757/221-0700, 470 McLaws Circle, www.courtyard.com, click on hotel directory, then Virginia, 151 rooms and 12 suites.

Pool, fitness center, tennis, spa (nearby), golf package. Two double bed guestroom runs from $140 to $170/per night.

Days Inn Colonial Resort, 720 Lightfoot Road, 888/563-4464, www.reservations.lodging.com, 120 rooms.

Pool, fitness center, further from Historic District, but near shopping outlets, golf and Busch Gardens. Under $100/night

Hampton Inn, 5 blocks from Historic District, 505 York Street, 757/220-3100, www.hampton.com,

Indoor pool, connecting rooms. There are two other Hampton Inns in the area, just a bit further from the Historic District. $120 for a two double-bed guest room.

I'm Hungry

Here are two delightfully colonial restaurants in the Historic District:

King's Arms Tavern $$, Duke of Gloucester Street, 757/229-1000.

Hearty colonial-era cuisine has you time travel back to the 18th century.

Chowning's Tavern $-$$, Duke of Gloucester Street at Queen Street, 757/229-1000.

Go on, live a little . . . in the past. Try the Welsh Rabbit in this reconstructed 1776 alehouse.

Where Are We Going Now?

Where are we going? Back in time. To the 1700s, when democratic ideals and revolutionary thoughts permeated the new society located right here in Williamsburg. Originally called Middle Plantation, the colony was established in 1633 to defend Jamestown. Williamsburg was the capital city of the Virginia colony, which in 1699 spread west to the Mississippi and north to the Great Lakes. Williamsburg lost its panache during the Revolutionary War, when political leaders fled to Richmond, a city much easier to defend.

Besides serving as a political center, Williamsburg also earned fame for its William and Mary College, established in 1693, the second-oldest college in the nation. From 1800 through the 1920s, Williamsburg enjoyed the perks attached to being an intellectual haven and a college town.

In 1926, Reverend Goodwin, rector of the Bruton Parish Church, persuaded John D. Rockefeller Jr., to restore Williamsburg to its colonial magnificence. Today, Williamsburg is the largest outdoor living-history museum. The 173-acre area includes 500 buildings, of which 88 are the original, and people dressed in 18th-century attire going about 18th-century business populate it.

Do not expect to cover Williamsburg in one day (that's why we've included several hotel recommendations). Stop at the Visitor's Center or check on-line for a map and pick the sites that most interested you and your family. Let your children have a vote. This is a democracy, you know!

Here are some highlights we recommend on your stroll down Duke of Gloucester Street:

The Capitol: The fiery Patrick Henry (1736-99) lambasted the Stamp Act in these corridors. The rather ornate building actually is a re-creation of the original structure, which went up in flames in 1753, only to have the second Capitol burn again in 1832. (Was Henry's revolutionary talk too fiery??) A 30-minute tour is available.

Blacksmith: Forging iron kept our children engaged for quite a while.

Printer's and Bookbinder's: Our children attended an art class once that allowed them to bind their own books. This shop was of particular interest to them as they compared notes with the costumed bookbinder.

Magazine and Guardhouse: On the south side of Market Square is the Magazine, one of the original structures at Williamsburg. Here is where colonialists would store arms and ammunition. Inside is a collection of period firearms. Next door is the guardhouse which was established during the French and Indian Wars.

Peyton Randolph House: off Gloucester on Nicholson. Mr. House was the first president of the Continental Congress. Walk north of the house to get an up-close look at a windmill (in operation in good weather) and the area where various Colonial trades are demonstrated.

Governor's Palace: The original burned down in 1781, but this re-creation does justice to the lavishness bestowed on the mansion that served as the British Crown's home-away-from-home in colonial Williamsburg. Once the royal governors bolted, Virginia's first two elected governors used the mansion: Patrick Henry and Thomas Jefferson.

A guide in full colonial garb conducts a tour of the Governor's Palace. After the tour, do let your children out into the gardens and maze. They are lovely and a fine opportunity to romp and play.

George Wythe House: Remember George (1726-1806)? He was the first Virginian to sign the Declaration of Independence. He also was law professor to the likes of Thomas Jefferson, John Marshall and Henry Clay.

BUSCH GARDENS

Thought you could travel to Williamsburg only for the history? Think again. Busch Gardens brings all time travelers back to the 21st Century – real fast. Want to speed down a track at 60mph? Or spin so fast you get the giggles? This is the place for you. It's a huge amusement park, with beautifully landscaped lawns. Lots of junk food, too. Sound like fun?

Busch Gardens is open from 10am to 10pm throughout the summer months (800/343-7946 or 757/253-3350). It closes earlier the rest of the year, and is not open at all November through February. One-day admission to Busch Gardens is a whopping $42.99 for adults and $35.99 per child (age 3-6). Ask for package deals at your hotel. There also is a package deal if you want to go to both Busch Gardens and Water Country USA (water park). Also check for late-day specials.

WATER COUNTRY USA

Hot, summer days cry out for a stop at Water Country USA (800/343-7946 or 757/253-3350). It's a blast –for parents, too. Tickets run $31.99 for adults and $24.99 for children (age 3-6). Remember, this is the land of deals, so check with your hotel, or arrange a package with Busch Gardens.

RESORTS

You've driven to D.C. with your family and now are looking for a fun way to drive back home. Well, if you're headed south, here are two fun family resorts where you can wander in the woods, tee up at a golf range or just breathe easy at the local spa. A journey far away from the penultimate spin city.

Wintergreen Resort, Wintergreen, Virginia, Route 664, 22958, 800/266-2444, info@wintergreenresort.com, www.wintergreenresort.com, from $165 in the lodge to $300 for a two-bedroom condo.

Directions: Take Route 66 out of Washington D.C. Exit at Rt. 29 south to I-64 west to Exit 107 (Crozet, Route 250). Take Route 250 west 5 mi. to Route 151 south, turn left. Follow Route 151 south 14 mi to Route 664. Turn right and Wintergreen is 4 miles ahead on Route 664.

Nestled in the Blue Ridge Mountains, we've made Wintergreen a family tradition for the 4th of July. Typically, this is the time of a music festival, culminating with fireworks rocketing off from the top of the ski slopes. The majestic mountains surrounding the resort simply add serenity to the festive fair of this summer, or any, holiday. Family Circle and Better Homes and Garden rated Wintergreen as one of the top family resorts in the U.S. Our kids will vouch for that!! They love the Treehouse children's program, which takes kids from 2 1/2 to 12 (half-day or full-day options are available, ranging from

$31 to $45, respectively), or for the Junior Explorer's program, for kids from 8 to 14 ($45/day). Your children also can choose to attend tennis camp. While the children are kicking up their heels in one of the many exciting adventures, you can hike on the Appalachian Trail, golf, play tennis, visit the newly expanded spa, or. . . just enjoy the mountain air. There are two lovely outdoor pools, one large enough for lap swimming, and an indoor pool for those rainy days.

The Homestead, Hot Springs, Virginia, stay@thehomestead.com, www.thehomestead.com, 800/838-1766. Rooms run from $260 and up, double occupancy.

Yes, it's almost heaven (and almost West Virginia). The morning mist ascending from the dark green treetops outside of your room is blissful. The afternoon tea, to the twinkling of the pianist in the grand hall after a long day's hike or river rafting, is pleasure itself. But, the rates will quickly bring you down to earth. Be prepared. Heaven comes at a price, but well worth it. We can't say enough about this resort. Its old-fashioned indoor bowling lanes, situated next to an invigorating mineral springs pool. The turn-of-the-century theater that runs evening movies. Spectacular hikes through nearby trails of the Allegheny Mountains. Each room is tastefully and elegantly appointed, yet children are quite welcome here. The Homestead offers today's guest a glimpse of the gracious past. In operation for over 200 years, The Homestead has been a home-away-from-home for many dignitaries, from George Washington to Bill Clinton. Enjoy dipping into the mineral waters at the nearby Jefferson Pools. And, don't forget the high quality children and teen programs.

If the price tag puts you off, but the heavenly environment keeps whispering in your ear, try staying at a nearby B&B (www.bbonline.com/va/hot+springs.html) or hotel (see www.expedia.com and type in Hot Springs, Virginia). You'll delight in the mountain atmosphere and give your pocketbook a break, too.

Chapter 9

I'M HUNGRY!

CAPITOL HILL

Monocle $$$, 107 D Street NE, 202/546-4488, Open Monday through Friday for lunch and dinner.

Crabcakes and politics. That's what you'll get at the Monocle, on the dining agenda for many Congressmen and women for the past 40 years. The Monocle is located a block from Union Station, just across the parking lot from the Dirksen and Hart Senate Office Buildings. While clearly geared for lobbyists on expense accounts, it serves up some of the best crab cake this side of Baltimore. Children less interested in the crab cake – and the political agenda – will be happy to know that the menu also includes hamburgers and other sandwiches. The Valonos family, owners of the restaurant, make dining at the Monocle a memorable experience for all.

Capital City Brewing Company $$, 2 Massachusetts Ave NE (in the National Postal Museum building, next to Union Station) and at 1100 New York Avenue NW (corner H and 11th), 202/842-BEER, www.capcitybrew.com. Open for lunch through dinner, Sunday to Thursday until midnight, Friday and Saturday until 2 a.m.

This faux-industrial beer-and-bratwurst house has a grilled sandwich for any appetite. As long as you are prepared to SPEAK UP over the din, your teens in particular will enjoy the hip, beer-soaked ambiance popular with the twenty-something Congressional staffers who flock here after work (or at least on Fridays after the boss is back in her district!). This place is a nice treat for beer lovers, since it has quite a good selection of microbrews. Perhaps the best touch and treat is the basket of warm, soft pretzels and spicy brown mustard brought out in place of bread. Burgers, chili and salad options complement the more noteworthy grilled sausage sandwiches.

America $$, Union Station, 2020-682-9555

The menu is HUGE. They have everything remotely American, from mash potatoes to quesadillas. And, while the food is not great, it's not bad either. You can sit out in the grand hall of Union Station, inside or, in good weather, even outdoors at a scattering of patio tables with a view of the Capitol Dome a short three blocks away. Our children enjoy sitting right outside America to see all the hustle and bustle of the lively train station.

Union Station Food Court $, 50 Massachusetts NE (lower level, beneath the grand hall), 202/371-9441. Most outlets open 10 a.m. to 9 p.m. on Monday through Saturday, and until 6 p.m. on Sunday.

Brother wants a burger. Sister only pizza. Dad prefers sushi. And mom just wants to settle the squabble (and grab Chinese or Indian). Solution: if you're near Capitol Hill, it's the Food Court below Union Station, which has all those fast food outlets and a dozen more. Seating is communal and plentiful – so split up and reconvene for eating.

If you want a step up from fast food, the concourse level has a number of different restaurants, from the eclectic America (see above), to Uno's Pizza, to a nice Tex-Mex restaurant (across from America, at the front entrance to Union Station), to Georgia Brown's, a rather fancy spread of southern and Cajun cuisine served up under some of most elaborate archways and woodwork in Washington. All of Union Station's restaurants are touristy, but none will leave you disappointed.

Take-out Time

Corner Bakery, Union Station, and at 529 14th Street NE, 202/371-8811.

The Corner Bakery is a great place for a quick breakfast of eggs or pastries, or for a carry-out lunch of subs, focaccio, or grilled cheese sandwiches. They have tables, but most of their business is carry-out. You can find Corner Bakery on the concourse (ground) level, in the extreme Southeast corner of the Station.

Eastern Market, 225 Seventh Avenue SE, Open Tuesday through Saturday from 7:30am to 3pm, Sunday 11am to 3:30pm.

Despite the crowds, Saturday mornings are the best time to visit Eastern Market. That's when the farmers come from as far as Pennsylvania to peddle fresh fruits and vegetables. The most popular draw, however, are the bargain breakfasts. If you don't mind waiting as long as 45 minutes in line, you can grab a heaping plate of blueberry-buckwheat pancakes for $4.00, or two eggs, grits and toast for a little less. You can take a seat, but don't tarry! Signs warn: "No saving seats, no reading newspapers, $100 fine for violations."

Yikes. We've only gone in great weather, when we can browse the fruit and snack stalls and sit outside.

DOWNTOWN

Galileo $$$$, 1110 21 Street NW 202/293-7191. Open Monday through Friday for lunch, daily for dinner.

As close to dining in the Piedmont area of Italy as you can get, Galileo is one of the top Italian restaurants in the country. Ingredients are as fresh as Roberto Donna, the celebrated chef, can get. This was Nancy Reagan's favorite restaurant for good reasons. Risotto with Parmesan (yum), halibut with porcini mushrooms (oh yes) and rockfish with braised fennel and red-pepper sauce (mouth-watering) are only a sampling of reasons to come to Galileo. Very posh, yet, it is Italian, so we vote for bringing well-behaved, well-dressed children.

Osteria Goldoni $$$$, 1120 20th Street NW 202/293-1511 Open Monday through Friday for lunch, daily for dinner.

Puglia's (southeastern Italy) culinary traditions are honored at Osteria Goldoni. Just the way mama made, try the tripe simmered in tomato sauce or the lamb stew with artichokes and olives. Let the little ones nibble off your plate and supplement their meal with pasta, plain and simple. Although this is perhaps our favorite Italian restaurant in D.C., like Galileo's it is very much a white linen table cloth affair.

Teatro Goldoni $$$, 1909 K Street NW 202/955-9494 Open Monday through Friday for lunch, Monday through Saturday for dinner.

Splendid, almost overwhelming, décor with food to match. Teatro Goldoni is a hip and elegant restaurant, but it is Italian, so bring the bambini. Try the roasted tomato, stuffed with artichokes, bread crumbs and mushrooms. Also tempting are the fish dishes – any of them! Like any of the three- and four-$ restaurants downtown, the kids should be nicely (even if casually) dressed and well-behaved, particularly during the regular lunch and dinner hours.

Café Atlantico $$$, 405 8th Street NW, 202/393-0812, Open Monday through Saturday for lunch, daily for dinner.

Cool and sleek. You expect – and you get – the young, single, beautiful people to wine and dine here. But so did our 10-year-old who really liked the lighting!! We brought Anthony here with us once before a performance at the Shakespeare Theater. He loved the guacamole and sweet potato sides – a meal enough for him. And, we enjoyed watching the effect of the classy environment. Perhaps school lunchrooms should be redesigned with soft lightening and relaxing, jazz music. PTA people, unite!

Taberna Del Alabardero $$$, 1776 I Street NW (enter on 18th Street between H and I Streets) 202/429-2200. Open Monday through Friday for lunch. Monday through Saturday for dinner.

You can almost hear the click-click of castanets and see the bull fights of yore in this authentic Spanish restaurant. Owner Luis Lezama also operates several restaurants in Spain. The menu frequently changes and daily specials are, well, changed daily. But, do look for the puchero – a soupy stew. It's filling for lunch.

The Prime Rib $$$, 2020 K Street NW 202/466-8811 Open Monday through Friday for lunch, Monday through Saturday for dinner.

Jacket and tie are required. Gorgeous flower arrangements placed in Chinese vases. Lovely brass lamps glow on each table. A pianist tickles the ivories at lunch and dinner. The waiters don tuxedos. Your three-year-old is screaming hysterically because their favorite cuddley was left behind. What's wrong with this picture?

If you have older children and you're a prime-rib kind-of-a person, do visit The Prime Rib. You can even order prime rib at lunch.

Luigino $$, 1100 New York Avenue NW (enter on H Street between 11th and 12th) 202/371-0595 Open Monday through Friday for lunch, daily for dinner.

Bobby Van's Steakhouse $$$, 809 15th Street NW 202/589-0060 Open Monday through Saturday for lunch, daily for dinner. Closed Sunday for lunch only.

Great steak, and all that goes with it like a splendid lobster cocktail. Bobby Van's also prepares excellent seafood, but why bother when you're here for the full monty of steak. Children who aren't big on meat can find a full compliment of baked or mashed potatoes, chicken and other more kid-friendly dishes.

Red Sage ($$ upstairs, $$$ downstairs), 605 14th Street NW, 202/683-4444.

Red Sage is two restaurants in one. The main floor combines a bar and family-priced Tex-Mex dining. Downstairs the pace is slower, with a menu boasting what you might call nouvelle Mexican – creative Southwestern cuisine with a flair for both the aesthetic and dramatic. Red Sage became famous during the first Bush administration, when 41 himself and top aides were spotted eating there on a regular basis. While there's no guarantee you'll see 43 or the First Lady there these days, the restaurant is just a short walk from the White House, Metro Center and the museums on the northeast side of the Mall (especially the American History and Natural History museums).

Old Ebbitt Grill $$, 675 15th Street NW, 202/347-4800.

You wouldn't be surprised to see the characters of West Wing rushing down a burger or steak in this historic watering hole less than a block from the White House. Dark wood paneling, gaslights and political bric-a-brac are the order of the day as you imagine – quite accurately – that those young suits with laminated badges dangling on chains from their necks are some of the President's or the Treasury Secretary's aides talking strategy over a beer and nachos after work. Luckily for families, this is also a fairly informal and affordable place (unlike the nearby Oval Room, or Hay Adams Hotel, White House haunts that cater strictly to Gucci-clad lawyers and lobbyists).

Bombay Palace $$, 2020 K Street NW 202/331-4200, Open daily for lunch and dinner.

One of the best Indian restaurants in Washington, Bombay Palace is understated elegance, but elegance none-the-less. This is a restaurant that enjoys children, as long as they are somewhat quiet! We review rules of behavior before entering and make sure we have keep-busy options like sketch pad and crayons, or books to read.

Try the tandoori specialties – out-of-this-world. Our children could gorge themselves on the freshly baked Indian bread, so we carefully and quietly delay and divvy up the bread. Barbara's favorite is the chickpea curry, while Michael has come back for more of the lamb vindaloo.

Malaysia Kopitiam $$, 1827 M Street NW 202/833-6232. Open daily for lunch and dinner. Dinner until 11pm Friday and Saturday (no wheelchair or stroller access).

Excellent and unique cuisine, Malaysia Kopitiam is a relaxed restaurant for families who are culinary adventurers. The owners, Leslie Phoon and chef Penny Phoon, won Washingtonian magazine's Restaurateur of the Year Award in 2002 for introducing diners to perhaps the least-known of Asian cuisines with "high quality, consistency and helpful guidance." A menu of 100 items comes along with an off-putting laminated binder with photos of each dish, so you will definitely know what you are getting. Leslie Phoon is a most gracious host and children are honored guests at Malaysia Kopitiam.

Our children love the fried bean curd. The Malaysian chili-shrimp is scrumptious. Or, a big bowl of soup – we love noodle soup with a hearty helping of stuffed vegetables.

Luigino $$, 1100 New York Avenue NW (entrance on H, between 11th and 12th Streets), 202/371-0595. Open daily for dinner, but only Monday through Friday for lunch.

Neighborhood Italian defines the cooking at Luigino. Scallopine, ravioli and just plain spaghetti will tempt your taste buds. The owner, Carmine Marzono, once was a chef at Galileo's, a premier D.C. Italian restaurant. And it shows. Luigino is less expensive, more child friendly, with ahh-now-that's-Italian food. The pizza is thin, crispy and light, one of the better ones in town.

Oodles Noodles $, 1120 19th Street NW 202/293-3138. Open Monday through Saturday for lunch and dinner. Sunday for dinner only.

Your little ones won't eat anything but noodles, but you're tired of spaghetti? Here's the place for you. You can order up just a bowl of plain noodles for them and treat yourself to excellent Asian cooking. Think Singapore, Hong Kong. The food here is authentic, well-prepared and served in a lovely Asian-décor café. Beware, however, lunch time is crunch time on week days at Oodles Noodles. Cheap and quick, the place is a favorite with paper pushers from blocks around. Try to time your stop just before or some time after the noon hour.

Star of Siam $, 1136 19th Street NW 202/785-2839, Open Monday through Saturday for lunch, daily for dinner.

We've always liked Thai restaurants. For a while, all our children would eat were noodles. Thai restaurants always have noodles dishes and usually are more than happy to serve little ones just a bowl of noodles. For you, however, the Star of Siam has much more. It's one of the best Thai restaurants in town. The curries are especially tasty. Try the yellow curry with shrimp, or the chicken with green curry.

Take-out Time

You can eat-in, too, at many of these restaurants.

Teaism $, 400 8th Street NW (near the MCI Center), 202/638-6010, and at 800 Connecticut Avenue NW (across Lafeyette Park from the White House), 202/835-2233. Open Monday through Friday for breakfast, lunch and dinner. Saturday and Sunday for brunch. Open Monday through Friday for breakfast, lunch and afternoon tea.

Asian cuisine and salads, soups and pre-prepared, but wonderful, sandwiches. Try the Thai chicken curry stir fry, or even the out-of-the-ordinary Ostrich Burger. Best of all, lots and lots of authentic tea carefully selected from across Asia. The connected Teaism store at the 8th Street location is a wonderful source for gifts. (See the longer description for the Teaism in DuPont Circle below).

BreadLine $, 1751 Pennsylvania Avenue, 202/822-8900, Open Monday through Friday until 3:30pm.

Stand in line for bread? You won't think it so strange once you've had a taste of Michael Furstenberg's old-fashioned, fresh-bread sandwiches. Furstenberg is of Marvelous Market fame – he started the original in Cleveland Park. Here he is now at one of the most popular luncheon eateries in D.C. Do brave the lines for one of his daily specials – more fresh than the packaged and refrigerated sandwiches. The BLTs are fantastic, topped of with real-potato french fries and you have a great lunch to go.

Corner Bakery $, 529 14th Street NW, or 1828 L Street NW, 202/347-8396/202/776-9052. Hours vary by location.

A good bet for a quick and inexpensive breakfast. See the description above for the Union Station location near Capitol Hill.

Ebbitt Express, $, 675 15th Street NW, 202/347-8881. Open Monday through Friday 7:30 a.m. to 5 p.m.

Simply a more limited version of the menu that day in the adjacent sit-down saloon of the Old Ebbit Grill (see the review above.)

CHINATOWN

Tony Cheng's Seafood Restaurant $, 619-621 H Street NW 202/371-8669, Open daily for lunch and dinner.

Tony Cheng's is a Chinatown landmark, rated best of breed among Chinese restaurants in the entire Washington area. A nice option for picky kids is to cook your own dish. No, really. At Tony Cheng's, guests can choose the Mongolian Hot Pot, where you, with the waiter offering suggestions, fill a hot pot with your own choice of ingredients. The restaurant is most appealing to true Chinese food enthusiasts. The menu is a virtual encyclopedia with dishes local to Hunan, Canton, Hong Kong and Szechuan prepared equally well. Adding to the aura of authenticity are the display cases of Dungeness crabs and Cantonese roast ducks (along the back wall). The portions are huge, so a family with younger kids can easily get by with one entrée less than the number of people.

Capital Q $, 707 H Street NW 202/347-8396. Open Monday through Saturday for lunch and dinner.

Yes, it's in Chinatown, but it is barbecue. Signed photos of Texas Republicans hang on the walls. YEEE, HAAA! Order up some of 'em spare ribs or brisket wrapped in a bun, tortilla or, hey, just eat it by itself. The peppery Elgin sausage imported from Texas are also recommended.

Eat First $, 609 H Street NW, 202/289-1703. Open daily for lunch and dinner, dinner served until 2a.m. Sunday through Thursday, and 3a.m. Friday and Saturday.

Chinese cooking at its best. The salt-water tank in the back means your seafood is as fresh as you can get. Try Eat First's famous shrimp cake with Chinese broccoli, once recommended to us by our waiter, and we have ordered it ever since.

Lei Garden $, 629-631 H Street NW 202/216-9696 Open daily for lunch and dinner.

You can choose to eat at the upstairs restaurant, or serve yourself at the downstairs buffet. The buffet ($8.95 during the week and $10.95 on weekends) is excellent, with hot and spicy stir-fried delights. Boiled dishes are good choices upstairs. The boiled curry of lamb (very spicy) and boiled fish filet are our favorites.

ESPN Zone: The Restaurant, $$, 555 12th St., Tel. 202/783-3776 .

A hotspot for kids who like to watch 17 TVs while they eat!! This is not the place for quiet conversation or family discussion. It's too loud. And, on every half hour, a sports minute is aired that will pump up your sports IQ (as you loose your hearing). Enough said about the noise. The food? It's actually good for a sports bar. You can choose, believe it or not, from some healthy items (like salads and salmon – look for the healthy foods tag) or real sports-lovers burgers. Enjoy!

Hard Rock Café, $$ 999 E St. NW, Tel. 202/737-7625.

Loud – real loud. Think ESPN Zone for hard rock lovers. And this café is packed with unbelievable rock-n-roll memorabilia – Bob Dylan's guitar, Keith Moon's buffalo-skin jacket and more. The place is filled with tourists. The food? At best unremarkable. Hamburgers are the most popular. But do step in to enjoy walk down memory lane and check out the momentos strung across the wall and hanging from the ceiling.

DUPONT CIRCLE

South of the Circle

I Ricchi $$$$, 1220 19th Street NW 202/835-0459. Open Monday through Friday for lunch, Monday through Saturday for dinner

We tried hard to maintain our life-before-children romance after Anthony was born. We once visited I Ricchi with little Anthony all decked out in a fancy baby outfit. Everyone oohed and ahhed over the cute child. Lucky for us, Anthony had developed this great habit of napping in restaurants. Michael laid him across his lap, Anthony would nod off, and we'd cover him gently with a napkin to avoid messy spills. Needless to say, we didn't return with children until they were able to behave like little adults (at least for an hour).

This is authentic Tuscan cuisine in a glamorous setting. The risottos and pastas are fresh, the sauces just right. Succulent wood-grilled fish and roasted meats make for a hearty fare. Enjoy a light desert – sorbet or biscotti – and dream lovely thoughts of the Tuscan hills.

The Palm $$$, 1225 19th Street NW 202/293-9091, Open Monday through Friday for lunch, daily for dinner.

Frequent business travelers know The Palm sets the standard for thick top-prime steaks, succulent (and gigantic!) lobsters and decadent cheesecake. Like the original Palm in Manhattan, this is the place to go for the very freshest and largest lobsters in town. If you don't mind an overdose of cholesterol, the Palm also is a place to see and be seen. It is a business-lunch landmark in Washington, D.C. and fun to visit to see if you know who's who in national legal and political circles.

Bacchus $$, 1827 Jefferson Place NW 202/785-0734, Open Monday through Friday for lunch and dinner and Saturday for dinner. Closed Sunday.

Lebanese cuisine means you can find something for everyone. Vegetarians are delighted with the hummos, mouth-watering baba ghanoush and other no-meat appetizers and entrees. Carnivores will love the lamb, chicken and other meat dishes. Your family might enjoy a mezza, which is a platter combining small portions of the many appetizers Bacchus has to offer. Best of all, Bacchus warmly welcomes children and families. Find Bacchus somewhat hidden down a flight of stairs on tiny Jefferson Place, a half block off Connecticut Avenue between M and N Streets.

Luna Grill & Diner, $$, 1301 Connecticut Avenue NW (next to the Starbucks at N Street), 202/835-2280. Open for lunch and dinner daily.

Luna is the place for a wide-variety of well-prepared sandwiches and salads. The burgers are fine, but we go there for a change of pace – like the sweet potato fries and the grilled portabello mushroom sandwich.

This is the sort of "health food" that the kids agree is cool. Eat inside or on the back patio, weather permitting. Very informal.

Al Tiramisu, $$, 2014 P St. NW, 202/467-4466.

We love this cozy, neighborhood Italian restaurant. It's cramped quarters and ultra-friendly service. From fresh fish to simple pastas, you can't go wrong. Our kids love the spinach-and ricotta-stuffed ravioli, with a brush of sage butter.

North of the Circle

Etrusco $$$, 1606 20th Street NW (facing Connecticut Avenue, at Q St.),202/667-0047. Open daily for dinner.

Barbara's 40th birthday party was held here, in the private room upstairs, with Michael deciding every last detail of the menu (including, of course, sea bass a la Calabrese!). It was grand. Ownership has changed several times, but we remain happy with the fare. With children, Etrusco is most appealing when the weather allows you to sit outside on the front patio, where they will be pre-occupied with the activity of bustling Dupont Circle. Etrusco features Tuscan cooking. We recommend the ribollita (bread, olive oil and shaved Parmesan swimming in a rich minestrone). Our children love this soup – a great way to disguise vegetables! Although Etrusco is elegant, it is also quite a bit more relaxed (and less expensive) than the four-star Galileo or Osteria Goldoni.

Lauriol Plaza $$, 1835 18th St. (at T St.), NW, 202/387-0035, Open daily from 11:30 am to 11 pm Sunday through Thursday, until midnight Friday and Saturday.

Lauriol Plaza is a three-tiered architectural paradise, tucked in an off-the-beaten-path neighborhood five blocks north of Dupont Circle, on the edge of Adams Morgan. It is a hopping place day and night. Try the rooftop terrace, especially pleasant during early evening hours in the summer. Tex-Mex reigns supreme, here. Try the cheese or beef quesadillas, the chiles rellenos, the beef quesadillas, and any of the mesquite-grilled specialties. Weekend brunch here is particularly popular with the singles who pack group houses and apartments in the Adams Morgan/DuPont area. It's very informal and friendly.

Teaism $, 2011 R Street NW (next door to Starbucks, ironically), 202/667-3827. Open daily from 8 a.m. to 10 p.m.

This is our children's favorite spot in Dupont Circle. It's where they learned to love tofu and tea! Their charming preschool, School for Friends, is located around the corner and Barbara has spent many a morning writing and editing her books right here, then picking up the children for a healthy snack. The menu is Asian ELABORATE, with a touch of the exotic (try the ostrich burger!). It is short-order cooking at its best. And it serves a wonderful breakfast, especially the French toast (weekends only) and the waffles (weekdays only). Teaism is also a serious tea house, selling dozens of green, black and white loose teas carefully selected from traditional sources across Asia. For serious advice on tea, ask for Linda, the owner, who is as friendly an expert as you could find.

Sit outside on the benches in good weather – or upstairs in the Spartan tea room other times. We always come equipped with sketch pads, books and . . . Okay, okay. Anthony and Carravita want readers to know about a fun game they play outside called "Hide the Straw." Simply get one of Teaism's little, black straws and hide it in plain view. Give hot and cold directions to the seeker. It has kept them engaged for hours, while we get time to relax and talk and sip our tea.

City Lights of China $$, 1731 Connecticut Avenue NW, 202/265-6688, www.citylightsofchina.com. Open weekdays and Sunday until 10:30 p.m., Saturday until 11 p.m.

By all accounts City Lights is the most popular Chinese restaurant in Washington outside of Chinatown. It is also informal enough to drop in on your sweaty way back from sightseeing (if the kids just can't wait) and will also deliver to hotels in the downtown area (if you can't). They have the usual wide variety of beef, lamb, chicken and duck entrees in various styles and degrees of spiciness. Among the more unusual dishes that rate rave reviews are the sizzling shrimp, orange beef and scallop & squid in spiced salt. Remember that there can be quite a wait after 7 p.m. on weekends. (Newly opened: A City Lights Express at the Ronald Reagan Center Food Court, 1300 Pennsylvania Avenue)

Typhoon $$, 2011 S Street NW (steps east of Connecticut Avenue), 202/667-3505. Open weekdays 11:30 am to 10:30 p.m., weekends until 11 p.m.

Typhoon's menu covers the whole range of classic Thai offerings, from satay and crispy tofu appetizers (our kids favorite), to chicken coconut soup (Tom Ka Gai), to Ka Pow seafood and crispy duck. Seafood lovers will be particularly pleased, since in addition to the usual stir fries and curries, Typhoon offers grilled salmon and tasty soft shell crabs. It's not as good as the popular Tara Thai, which is in downtown Bethesda, but considering the price and relaxed atmosphere it's a convenient choice downtown.

Kramerbooks and Afterwards Cafe $$, 1517 Connecticut Avenue NW (between DuPont Circle and Q Street). www.kramerbooks.com. Open daily until 1 a.m.

We all love to browse at Kramerbooks, a very hip and high-brow bookstore with a very informal café in back. Sometimes we come only for a snack (yummy deserts) or a drink. But lunch and dinner are fine, too. The selection is good, the food okay, the children love to read their latest purchases and we get a little one-on-one time! Heaven.

Zorba's Café $, 1612 20th St, NW (facing Connecticut Avenue, at Q St.), 202/387-8555, www.ZorbasCafe.com. Open Mon. through Sat. 11 a.m. until 11:30 p.m., Sundays until 10:30 p.m.

Another quick and inexpensive sit-down-or-carry-out option is Zorba's. As the name suggests, it's all the Greek you can eat: hummos, falafel, kebabs and, of course, gyros (called yeros here). The vegetarian platter is great way to sample (or share) small portions. Michael loves the chicken souvlaki, which he often grabs as a carry-out. Zorba's is fast and informal since, like Midi, you order at the counter and carry your tray to a table inside or out front. In nice weather it's a particularly good spot for lunch, since the patio looks out over the bustle of DuPont Circle.

Take-out Time

Julia's Empanadas $, 1221 Connecticut Avenue NW and 1410 U Street, NW (two of the four locations in NW Washington), 202/861-8828. Open daily until 11 p.m.

Owner William Hohman lovingly calls them "poor people's food," but at roughly $3 a pop his home-baked empanadas have become quite a hit among the young and restless in NW Washington. Like the Polish (who love their pierogi) and the Italians (who scarf calzones), in Latin America the concept of a baked crust filled with meat, cheese, beans, or whatever turns you on has spread to El Norte. Of course, quick, cheap and tasty are the attributes that will appeal to families on the go. You can even tempt the kids with a fruit-filled empanada for dessert!

Marvelous Market $, 1511 Connecticut Avenue NW 202/331-3690.

Steps north of DuPont Circle and next door to Kramer Books is one of the few gourmet and European-style groceries in Washington. Marvelous Market is a great place to outfit a picnic or to pack a lunch. The breads and sandwiches are fresh from their bakery, the fruits are flawless and the salads and other ready-made sides are tasty. It is also a good place to grab pastries for breakfast (the cheese Danish is lush), as is the Firehook bakery just around the corner on Q Street.

GEORGETOWN

Michel Richard Citronelle $$$$, Latham Hotel, 3000 M Street NW, 202/652-2150, Open Monday through Friday for lunch, daily for dinner.

Modern French cuisine. Chi chi to the max. A seven-course degustation menu. When a restaurant is named for its famous chef, you know it's going to be a special meal. Pricey, but certainly one of the best dining experiences in this country. Bring the kids? Not the young ones; but maybe for teens who appreciate nouvelle cuisine.

Café Milano $$$$, 3251 Prospect Street NW, 202/333-6138, Open Monday through Friday for lunch, daily for dinner

We hear it's the "in" restaurant, then we hear it's "out." Who knows! All we can say is that when it's "in" it has been a haunt for the likes of Michael Jordan and other D.C. celebrities. But it also has prices that go hand-in-hand with being a celebrity hang out. Pizzas are good, but do you really want to spend almost $100 on a few individual-sized pizzas and drinks? It's a great atmosphere, but try it without the kids.

Sequoia $$ to $$$, 3000 K Street NW, Washington Harbor Complex (on the Potomac), 202/944-4200. Open for lunch and dinner daily and brunch on Saturday and Sunday.

Dashing from monument to monument all day? Spending six or more hours in even some of the world's best museum can be enough to make your head spin. Want a breath of fresh air? Stunning view? OK food?

Then take your family to Sequoia, situated in a prime location on the waterfront in Georgetown – at least on a day nice enough to dine outdoors. Dazzling pink sunsets reflect off the Potomac. As daylight fades, the lights of the pier come to life, creating a new fanfare of lights dancing on the river. Seated outdoors on the large tiered patio, your children have more wiggle room and their squeals of fun blend into the cacophony of a buzzing waterfront restaurant. As you gaze across at the Kennedy Center, you also get to people watch, since the Sequoia has a quite hip bar where all the beautiful people without children go!

Oh yes, the food. Unremarkable, but it's a menu with lots and lots of choices. Combine several appetizers – chicken empanada, calamari, guacamole or Ceasar salad. They also have a raw bar of shrimp, lobster, oysters. The usual suspects are available for children – hamburgers, pasta and pizza. Try their gazpacho soup – not too spicy, our children enjoyed it in the heat of the summer.

Tony & Joe's $$ to $$$, 3000 K Street NW, Washington Harbor Complex (on the Potomac), 202/944-4545.

Sit outside if you can (steps from Sequoia, in fact). The river view is stunning, and your youngest of children will delight in the dancing waterfall fountain nearby. We spent many an evening with Anthony and Carravita

166 WASHINGTON, D.C. WITH KIDS

walking around this masterpiece of cascading, jumping, bouncing water, looking for some of the ducks who take up summer residence here. It's a fantastic diversion. Sundays are Jazz Brunch days from 11am to 3pm ($26 for adults, $16 for children).

Fish is king at Tony & Joe's, although meat eaters will find a few choice dishes, too. Start off with the piping hot crab dip served with French bread croutons. Try the grilled tuna or the crab-stuffed flounder.

1789 Restaurant $$$, 1226 36th St. NW (adjacent to the Georgetown University campus), 202/965-1789. Open daily for lunch and dinner; no stroller or wheelchair access.

If you want a taste of upscale colonial era cuisine served in a rustic old federal townhouse, this is the place. This would be a perfect stop for parents with teens checking out the campus and interested in the historical aspects of Georgetown. The food is quite appealing as well, most notably the rack of lamb, the Portuguese seafood stew and the perennial pine-nut-crusted chicken breast. Make reservations far in advance for a weekend evening or brunch, particularly when the University is in session.

Clyde's $$$, 3236 M Street NW, 202/333-9180. www.clydes.com. Open for lunch and dinner until 3 a.m. Fridays and Saturdays and until 2 a.m. other nights.

Definitely make a reservation if you are determined to eat during prime time at this very popular and informal saloon – the original location of what has become a chain catering to all ages. The kids will love their "Busy Bag" with crayons and coloring book to keep them busy while parents scan the very familiar American menu that includes burger platters, omelettes, soups and salads. Clyde's also boasts one of Washington's most trifling historical artifacts: in the Patio Room you can see the Gold record awarded to the Starland Vocal Band for their hit "Afternoon Delight," allegedly inspired by the same-named snack menu at Clyde's. Now that's history.

Café La Ruche $$, 1039 31st Street NW, 202/965-2684.

Café La Ruche is the pot of gold at the end of the rainbow. For good behavior, promise your children a visit to this charming French café steps from the C&O Canal in the heart of Georgetown. Why? To pick one of the many whipped-cream topped pastries from a dessert case to die for. You also can get sandwiches, soup, salad and an oversized cappuccino. Walk through the café to the small outdoor garden and enjoy a wonderful afternoon just off the busy streets of Georgetown. This place is a favorite with local families of all ages, particularly for Sunday brunch, when the wait for a table can be an hour or more. No reservations accepted.

Bistro Francais $$, 3124-28 M Street NW, 202/338-3830, Open daily for lunch and dinner.

A neighborhood landmark since the 1970s, Bistro Francais is good value for the money. A relaxed, hang-out sort of atmosphere, it's in a prime

Georgetown location. Our children love the potato gratin. The cuisine is typical and well-prepared French fare, with lots of selections. Enjoy.

Amma Vegetarian Kitchen $, 3291 M Street NW, 202/625-6625. Open daily for lunch and dinner until 10 p.m.

Indian cooking at its best – and at a considerably cheaper price than the pretentious (though superb) Heritage India (in the Glover Park section of Georgetown, at 2400 Wisconsin Avenue, 202/333-3120). What sets Amma apart, as its name implies, is its strictly vegetarian kitchen – meaning no meat, fish or even eggs. Our children love the cream-sauce vegetarian meatballs. The curries are freshly prepared – though be sure to ask which ones might be too spicy for children unaccustomed to eating Indian cuisine. One excellent curry popular with our son is the aviyal, which is mixed vegetables in coconut sauce.

Dean & DeLuca $, 3276 M Street NW, 202/342-2500.

Imported from New York City, Dean & DeLuca gives new meaning to upscale shopping. This is the Versace of grocery stores. Right outside the store, snuggled between it and the Georgetown Park shopping mall, is the Dean & DeLuca café. Salads of all sorts, deserts, soups, exotic drinks, as well as good cappuccino and hot chocolate. We have spent many a Sunday afternoon brunching here after long hikes along the C&O Canal path that runs just behind this gourmet snack stop. Check out their gelato!!

Pizzeria Uno $, 3211 M Street NW (also in Cleveland Park, at 3300 Connecticut Ave NW, and at Union Station), 202/965-6333. Open daily for lunch through dinner, until 10 p.m.

All kinds of pizzas, salads, drinks. This chain is famous for its Chicago-style pan pizza (although they have thin crust as well). Your kids might not even mind eating their vegetables when they are packed in cheese on a "spinoccoli" or "shroom" pizza. A fun-loving pizza place for families. Very informal; no reservations accepted.

Prospects $, 3203 Prospect Street, 202/298-6800, Open lunch and dinner Tuesday through Saturday. Closed Sunday and Monday.

New-age pizza, but the old standards are still there.

Take-out time

Fresh Fields $, 2323 Wisconsin Avenue, 202/333-5393.

The famously healthy supermarket has plenty of picnic supplies and an informal place to munch on deli delights.

CLEVELAND PARK/WOODLEY PARK

Lebanese Taverna $$, 2641 Connecticut Avenue NW, 202/265-8681, Open Monday through Saturday for lunch, daily for dinner.

Lebanese Taverna is a good choice after a trip to the zoo, as it is across the street from the Woodley Park/National Zoo Metro station (Red line), one among six otherwise touristy restaurants across from the enormous Sheraton Washington Hotel. Lebanese Taverna is relaxed, although not enough to show up in T-shirts and shorts for dinner. Nevertheless, this is a wonderfully family-friendly restaurant and perhaps the best middle-eastern kitchen in town. The humus is heavenly. Kabobs, superb. The musakaa a special treat. But watch out for those chick peas. Once, baby Anthony started flicking his chick peas when one took off, bouncing off the back of a gentleman's head. "Huh?" he said, looking around in disdain. "Ohhhhh," we exclaimed, failing miserably to control our laughter. Once he caught on that a one-year-old was the culprit, all was well.

Cactus Cantina $, 3300 Wisconsin Avenue, 202/2686-7222, Open daily for lunch and dinner.

Let's see. How can we best recommend this restaurant. Suffice it to say that each year, every year for the past six years our children have chosen Cactus Cantina as the restaurant to celebrate their birthday. Could it be the guacamole? The quesadillas? The coloring book each child get? The chance to watch the fresh-baked tortillas roll out of the oven as inflated little pillow puffs? How about the flan or coconut ice cream balls draped with caramel sauce? Or the way the staff sings Happy Birthday when bringing out the dessert, candle flaming (we wonder what happened to the sparklers)?

This is a festive and fun, not fancy, Tex-Mex restaurant, with outdoor seating that loops around the restaurant. A great place to stop after a visit to the National Cathedral, as it is just two blocks further north.

2 Amys Pizza $, 3715 Macomb St, NW (just off Wisconsin, next door to Cactus Cantina).

The pizza pies here are a big hit with kids and parents alike. We're not talking Domino's – this is authentic, Neapolitan-style pizza cooked in a wood-fired oven. The owners consciously aspire to make the best and most traditional pizza this side of the Atlantic. Families we know love this place, although it is often so crowded in the evenings that we end up next door in Cactus Cantina, to our children's delight. Thus, if you are determined to discover how different true Italian pizza tastes from the greasy, cardboard takeout variety, come for a late lunch or before 6 p.m. The restaurant is a short walk north from National Cathedral.

Take-out Time

Vace Italian Deli $, 3315 Connecticut Avenue NW, 202/363-1999, and in downtown Bethesda at 4705 Miller Ave., 301/654-6367. Monday through Saturday to 8 p.m.

Although there's nary an Italian in sight, the pizza is cheap, tasty and sold by the slice. Italian subs, cannoli (pastry shells filled with sweet ricotta cheese filling) and a wide selection of imported Italian specialty items round out the menu.

BETHESDA & CHEVY CHASE, MARYLAND

Thyme Square Café, 4735 Bethesda Ave., Bethesda (one block west of Wisconsin Ave.), Tel. 301/657-9077. Open daily for lunch and dinner until 10pm, Friday and Saturday nights until 11pm. $$$

Healthy food never had it so good. Although you won't find red meat on the menu, you won't miss it either, particularly if you enjoy seafood. The Brazilian seafood stew is to die for, with its spicy broth chock full of shellfish and flavored with coconut milk and plantain fries. All the seafood is good, if expensive. Veggies, of course, have no end of options. Our favorite appetizer by far is the wood-roasted stuffed artichoke – you may not even realize you like artichoke until you've dipped the leaves in this tangy sauce. The pizzas are small, but a tasty and less pricey option for kids. Thyme Square is a very friendly, informal atmosphere; and you can dine on the patio, weather permitting.

Café Deluxe, 4910 Elm St., Betehsda (just off Old Georgetown Road), Tel. 301/656-3131. Also located in D.C., near National Cathedral at 3228 Wisconsin Ave. NW. Open daily for lunch through dinner, 11:30am to 10:30pm. $$-$$$

You won't be the only family with young children at this eclectic American bistro. Café Deluxe has something for everyone, from grandma (meatloaf, her roasted chicken) to funky Aunt Patty (roasted lamb and goat cheese sandwich, red pepper humus rolls). And don't worry, the kids can always have pizza (again). We've found that sharing several side dishes such as the grilled asparagus, fresh snap peas and garlic mashed potatoes – is a good approach to this mostly a la carte menu.

Tara Thai $$, 4828 Bethesda Ave., Bethesda (two blocks west off Wisconsin Avenue), 301/657-0488. Open daily for lunch and dinner until 10 pm.

Families flock to Tara Thai, perhaps the most popular Asian restaurant around. It's partly the reasonable prices and relatively quick service. It's partly the baby blue murals of dolphins and other sea creatures swimming whimsically across the walls. And it's partly the consistent competence of the kitchen serving up all the standard Thai favorites. As the décor suggests, the seafood is especially good, particularly the Typhoon soup, soft-shell crabs and Deep Sea shellfish stew. Our kids make a meal out of the golden-fried tofu. If you are in a hurry, it's a good bet for carry-out as well.

Rio Grande Café $$, 4949 Fairmont Ave., Bethesda (just off Old Georgetown Road), 301/656-2981. Open daily for lunch through dinner until 11:30 pm week nights and until 11:30 pm on Friday and Saturday.

This is Bethesda's version of D.C.'s popular Cactus Cantina (reviewed above under Woodley/Cleveland Park). It's Tex-Mex, noisy and thus perfect camouflage for antsy eight-year-olds. The tortilla machine is a curiosity the kids will enjoy, as the parents douse the fires of a hot day trudging the Mall with a frozen marguerita. Portions are large and prices are moderate, so the only obstacle to flan for dessert is eating too many of the fresh warm chips and guacomole before the fajitas or other entrees arrive. One warning: On weekends the wait can be an hour or more at dinner time.

Pines of Rome $$, 4709 Hampden Lane, Bethesda (just off Wisconsin Ave, downtown Bethesda), 301/657-8775. Open for lunch through dinner until 10 pm Sunday and Monday, 11 pm Tuesday through Saturday.

Pines is a favorite of local families, as it is one of the oldest, fastest and least expensive Italian restaurants in the Washington area (with locations in DuPont Circle and suburban Virginia as well). Pines is peasant food. People come here to stuff hungry kids with big appetites at affordable prices. The white pizza is famous, although for our money the basic spaghetti dishes, such as spaghetti carbonara, are safe bets as well. Pines is charming; if you want a dining experience, try Francesco Ricchi's **Cesco** in Bethesda's restaurant district.

Matuba $$, 4918 Cordell Ave., Bethesda, 301/652-7449. Open Monday through Saturday for lunch through dinner.

Sushi on steroids. Matuba has a long menu of all the traditional sushi favorites, from mackeral to squid to amberjack. It sports a regulaton sushi bar, as well as tables in airy small rooms on split levels. The basic Japanese-American standards are here as well, including teriyaki (chicken and beef) and tempura (shrimp and vegetable). If your kids will eat this sort of food, Matuba is a rated a best bargain.

Original Pancake House $, 7700 Wisconsin Ave., Bethesda, 301/986-0285 (also at 12224 Rockville Pike, Rockville, MD, 301/468-0886). Open daily for breakfast through dinner.

Breakfast anyone? This is a favorite among the local soccer moms (and dads) and on Saturdays you'll certainly end up in line behind kids in cleats and colorful jerseys. Everyone knows what to expect at a pancake house, but one specialty that sets this place apart is the excellent (and gigantic!) baked apple pancake. A combination of Granny Smith apples, cinnamon and syrup can easily feed two (adults or kids) for under $10. The regular pancakes are as fluffy as the atmosphere is kid-friendly. So, for a change, sit down for breakfast.

OLD TOWN ALEXANDRIA AND ARLINGTON, VIRGINIA

Blue Point Grill $$$ to $$$$, 600 Franklin St., Alexandria (Old Town), 703/739-0404. Open daily for lunch and dinner.

If you are a seafood lover, or just in the mood for relaxed, upscale dining, Blue Point Grill is one of the most highly rated restaurants in northern Virginia. On a warm evening the patio is an inviting spot for families with young children. Even inside, the restaurant is far from stuffy, although it sports the sort of understated elegance the grandparents would love. Start with the raw bar sampler – oysters, clams, mussels and shrimp cocktail – and wash it down with a delightful Belgian beer ominously called Delirium Tremens! The entrees are as creative as they are fresh, including scallop mousse with lobster, chilled lobster with champagne, and horseradish-crusted sea bass. Anthony and Carravita's grandma, who is not so adventurous, was perfectly content with the pan-roasted halibut. Michael recommends the lobster mashed potatoes – as much for novelty as taste! For dessert, indulge the Dolly Sin fudge cake or fall back on the home-made ice cream. Bon appetit.

Generous George's Positive Pizza & Pasta Place $$, 3006 Duke St., Alexandria, (locations also in Annandale and Springfield, VA), 703/370-4303. Open daily from 11 am until 10 pm, except Friday and Saturday nights until 11 pm.

They could simply have named this place Generous George's Pizza Palace. Pizza, pizza everywhere. Everything from the décor to the pasta is served up as pizza. As well it should, since the pizza crust here is fabulous – puffy, crispy, light and chewy all at once. And the toppings are generous indeed. Try the fennel-flavored sausage, Canadian bacon and Genoa Salami, ideally all together if you are a real meat lover. Personal pizzas are the best bargain, but available only during the week at lunch.

Monroe's American Trattoria $$, 1603 Commonwealth Ave., Alexandria, VA, 703/548-5792. Open daily for dinner from 5 pm until 10 pm, except on Friday and Saturday nights until 11 pm and Sunday until 9 pm. Also open for Sunday brunch, 9:30 am until 2 pm.

Monroe's is basic, not exceptional, Italian food. But it wins great praise for pampering the bambini. You won't have to chase after the hostess for a highchair, since the seating (and coloring) needs of your half-pints will be anticipated in advance. All ages enjoy Monroe's, and indeed you'll be as likely to see a retired couple as you will young families and young couples. The spaghetti marinara is a safe bet for kids, as always, as is the pizza (which is filling, but nothing special). One unusual specialty to try if it's on the menu is the pizzocheri, a hearty mix of buckwheat noodles, potatoes and Swiss chard flavored with gorgonzola cheese, garlic, butter and sage. Very satisfying.

Stella's $$, 1725 Duke St., Alexandria, 703/519-1946. Open daily for lunch, from 11:30 am to 2:30 pm, and for dinner from 5 pm until 10 pm, except Sunday when it closes at 9:30.

Bring the grandparents. Stella's is a very welcome throwback to the great American diners of the 1940s. Named after Stella Dallas, the title role played so fetchingly by Barbara Stanwyck in the 1937 movie classic, Stella's is decorated with murals of returning World War II soldiers and other momentoes of that era. The menu is a classy remake of all the old favorites: a generous New York strip steak, burgers (the Black Angus) and a variety of sandwiches. Try the excellent smoked and peppered roast beef sandwich. A competent selection of microbrews rounds out the menu.

Five Guys $, 107 N. Fayette Street, Alexandria, VA (Old Town), 703/549-7991. Open daily from 11 am until 10 pm.

Burger heaven, pure and simple. Local hamburger addicts drive miles to eat here. Even Texans rave. This place wins no points for ambiance; it's institutional red-and-white tile seems designed mainly to make it easy to sweep up the peanut shells (large brown sacks of which are available for munching while you wait). The french fries are the best around, hand cut and cooked in peanut oil. And the burgers weigh in at under $4. If you want the complete experience, order the bacon cheeseburger with everything – unless you don't like A-1 sauce, hot sauce and jalapeno peppers on your burger, in which case you can be choosey. (Hey, has anyone introduced the 2 Amys in Cleveland Park to the Five Guys in Alexandria?)

Los Amigos $, 703 King St., Alexandria (Old Town), 703/548-8078. Open daily for lunch, from 11:30 am until 2:30 pm, and daily for dinner until 10 pm, except Friday and Saturday nights until 11 pm.

By Old Town standards, Los Amigos is a family friendly bargain. All the usual Mexican food favorites. Although be careful not to over-order; the chips and salsa are so good that we are often half-full before the sides of guacamole arrive! Extremely casual.

Sala Thai $, 2900 N. Tenth St., Arlington, 703/465-2900 (also in D.C. at 2016 P St. NW, 202/872-1144). Open for lunch and dinner daily.

Cheap, quick and delicious, Sala Thai is a favorite among locals on a budget. The extensive menu offers all the Thai options you would expect, and then some. We particularly enjoy the tom ka gai soup (a spicy chicken and coconut-flavored soup) and the satays.

Clarendon Grill $, 1101 N. Highland St., Arlington, VA, 703/524-7455, www.cgrill.com. Open for lunch and dinner daily until 11 pm.

Although this becomes a party-place for the twenty-somethings as the evening wears on, it will definitely please your teens. The wraps and sandwiches here are excellent and under $10. Our favorites include the Colorado Turkey Sandwich (smoked turkey and Jack on sourdough) and the Philly Sandwich (cheese smothering steak, mushrooms and onions on a baguette). There is live music on the weekends and free salsa lessons on Monday nights at 7:30. Cha-cha-cha!

Rhodeside Grill $, 1836 Wilson Blvd., Arlington, VA, 703/243-0145, www.rhodesidegrill.com. Open for breakfast through dinner daily.

If you need breakfast or brunch in Arlington, this would be the place. Belly up to the omelet station and have it your way. Fresh waffles, fruit, home fries and other choices are included in the $9 all-you-can-eat brunch buffet. Beyond breakfast, Rhodeside has respectable burgers and a very nice chicken BLT sandwich, among other classics.

Chapter 10

WHICH ONE IS MY ROOM?

Hotels abound in Washington, mainly due to a high level of tourism and numerous business conventions. While you certainly can find incredibly luxurious hotels – the Hay Adams and the Four Seasons, to name two – many more economical hotels also exist sawith fun amenities for families also exist.

One critical **money saving tip**: **Check in on Friday**. The rates are considerably lower over the weekend. Hotel staff at many of the hotels listed here informed us that rates are higher during the week because of the many business travelers, whose companies foot the bill. The "leisure" traveler gets to save beaucoup bucks if he or she checks in on Friday, when most business people leave.

Another tip: **always ask for the family rate**. While not all hotels have special rates, you will never know unless you ask. We also have found that rates fluctuate from season to season. So don't be shy to ask for the best deal.

Most hotels will allow up to four, in some cases five, people to stay in one room to accommodate families. Do ask about connecting rooms, if you need more space. **Beware**, however, **several hotels said they could not guarantee connecting rooms**. When you reserve connecting rooms, get a clear response as to whether or not they will guarantee connecting rooms for your family.

Also, parents looking for **babysitting, be aware of extra charges**, which quickly add up. The going rate is $10/hour. But the firms the hotels contract with usually require a four-hour minimum, transportation charge (about $12) and extra fee for more than one child. Many of the larger hotels provide baby-sitting services, and we've noted them. But remember to check on the availability of child-care when you make reservations.

Other **hidden charges** include hotel tax, which amount to about another $15 per night, and parking, which can run as high as $20 a night.

Some hotels provide **Internet specials**. Quite frankly, we've found you often can get similarly low rates by negotiating over the phone. But check these Internet sites just in case:

• www.washington.org – the official web site of the D.C. Convention and Visitor's Association. Hotels, B&Bs and hostels are searchable by price and location. A good site.
• www.priceline.com – we didn't like the fact that you can't get enough information about the hotel – like location! — until you book a room. If you need more info before you book the room, just call directory assistance (202/555-1212) to get the hotel's number or search on-line for the hotel's direct web address.

Parent Tip

Go to the search engine www.google.com and type in the hotel name and city). If all is well, then summon up priceline.com and book.

• www.preferredhotels.com – controlled by the hotel industry's Travelweb.
• www.washingtonpospt.com – the city's newspaper offers a search engine to find hotels by location and price.

Non-smoking rooms are almost always available. Make sure hotel staff can guarantee you a smoke-free room upon your arrival.

To guide you with your hotel selection, we've used these categories:
• **Very Expensive** – over $200
• **Expensive** — $150-$200
• **Moderate** — $100-150
• **Inexpensive** – Under $100

The rates we note here are based on double occupancy; children are almost always free.

Remember, because of Washington's excellent Metro system and the relatively inexpensive cost of taxis, renting a car is unnecessary and ill advised. Driving is chaotic, parking is limited and parking tickets frequent and expensive. Rent a car for field trips outside of Washington only.

Enjoy finding a cozy room for your visit to Washington!

CAPITOL HILL

Very Expensive

Hyatt Regency Washington, 400 New Jersey Avenue, 202/737-1234 or 800/2133-1234, Fax 202/737-5773, www.regencywashington.com. 802 units, Babysitting: ask the concierge, Rates: $240 to $315, Restaurant: Park Promenade (breakfast, lunch – great buffet, dinner), Capitol View Club (dinner on the rooftop), Metro: Union Station.

We love the lobby – a five-story atrium makes it so open and airy. The Hyatt is the home of many political events, but it also is a good bet for tourists, located just two blocks from the Capitol and the Mall. Children love the large, indoor pool, but you must be on the hotel's business plan to have access. There also is a health club for business plan members. Rooms are well appointed and large enough for a family of four to live comfortably for a few days.

Phoenix Park Hotel, 520 North Capitol Street NW, 202/638-6900, 800/ 824-5419, Fax 393-3236, phoenixpark@worldnet.att.net. 150 units, Babysitting: no, Rates: $215-$340 for a double room, Restaurant: The Dubliner, lunch and dinner, Metro: Union Station (across the street)

Even if you don't stay here, come to the Dubliner – a real Irish pub. A century ago, the neighborhood around Union Station was a poor, Irish ghetto. Fish and chips, shepherd's pie and IRISH MUSIC!! You'll join many Hill staffers here. The hotel is Old World Celtic charm. Each room is well appointed and makes you think you're spending the night in Ireland's countryside. You are steps from the Capitol and very close to the Mall. Remember Tip O'Neil, the famous Speaker of the House? He partied here for his 80th birthday. So "Cead Mile Failte" – A hundred thousand welcomes. Enjoy a wee-bit-of-the Irish (and even a fitness center) at the Phoenix Park.

Expensive

Hotel George, 15 E Street NW, 800/576-8331 or 202/347-4200, Fax 202/347-4213, www.hotelgeorge.com. 147 units, Babysitting: yes, Rates: Weekday from $220 and weekend from $149, Restaurant: Bis (breakfast, lunch, dinner), Metro: Union Station.

Staid and true George W. (Washington, that is) may have found Hotel George perplexing. The geometric lines, and feng shui décor are a far cry from colonial Mt. Vernon. But the recently renovated hotel gets high points for being hip. The lobby gleams in glass and stainless steel. Guest room décor is minimalist. If you're trying to impress your teens, it's the place for you. The restaurant, Bis, is one of the best — and by far the hippest – on the Hill; the cuisine is nouveau Italian.

Holiday Inn on the Hill, 415 New Jersey Avenue, 202/638-1616, 800/638-1116, www.basshotels.com/holiday-inn. 350 units, Babysitting: can make arrangements, also hotel has a Discovery Zone for children 4-12, Rates: $100 to $215, Restaurant: (breakfast, lunch, dinner), Metro: Union Station

HI on the Hill is the Holiday Inn. Typical American décor, but comfortable rooms in a great location. Enjoy the rooftop pool and patio. Most interesting for families is the Discovery Zone – a fun room for children between the ages of 4 to 12. Discovery Zone is open from June through August 4pm to 10pm, just long enough for you to have a leisurely dinner. The room is filled with computers, a television, games and toys. A qualified staff person keeps the children content while you have an adults night out.

Moderate

Capitol Hill Suites, 200 C Street NW, 202/543-6000, 800/424-9165, 152 suites, Babysitting: no, Rates: $100-$250, Restaurant: none, but there is a continental breakfast and lots of cafes and restaurants nearby, Metro: Capitol South.

Located on the House of Representatives side of the Capitol, this is a good find for Capitol Hill. Most of the rooms have a kitchen and dining room and you can have access to a nearby health club. Close to the Mall.

Best Western Capital Skyline, 10 I Street SW, 202/488-7500 or 800/458-7500, Fax 202/488-0790, 203 units, Babysitting: no, Rates: from $119, some connecting rooms, Restaurant: breakfast, lunch, dinner, Metro: Union Station

Good place to hang your hat while you spend the day touring. Nothing fancy, but there is an outdoor pool and a parking garage – no charge! It's five blocks from the Capitol, further to the Mall. Be attentive walking the streets at night since the area south of the Hill clears out after work.

DOWNTOWN

Very Expensive

Hay Adams, 800 16th Street, 202/638-6600, 800/853-6807, www.hayadams.com. 145 guestrooms, Babysitting: can make arrangements, Rates: $249 (Queen bedroom), $715-$775 (junior suite), Restaurant: Lafayette Room Metro: Metro Station.

When your neighbor is the president of the United States, how can you go wrong? The Hay Adams recently renovated its elegant hotel, which is now even more stunning. New linens drape the beds, décor is lavish with ornamental fireplaces and tapestries throughout. Your stay certainly will be comfortable, with the standard room large enough to hold a family of four. Enjoy tea and a view of the White House. Rooftop dining awards you with a panoramic view of Washington, especially gorgeous at night. If you want to spend this kind of money, however, we suggest you stay at the Four Seasons in Georgetown, which appears to be much more child friendly.

Grand Hyatt Washington at Washington Center, 1000 H Street NW, 800/233-1234 or 202/582-1234, Fax 637-4781, www.washington.grand.hyatt.com. 960 units. Babysitting: can make arrangements, Rates: Family plan $320, connecting room an additional $150, but check the Internet for cheaper fares and ask for summer deals, Restaurants: Grand Café (open 6:30 to 3:00), Via Pacifica (open 5pm to 10pm), Zepher Deli (open 6:30am to 3pm) and the Grand Slam Sports Bar (open 11am to midnight), Metro: Metro Center.

Gorgeous hotel, but look out for extra charges. There is an indoor pool and health club, but its $10 unless you are at the Regency- or business-plan level. The family plan does give you a children's menu and children-size portion and prices at the hotel's restaurants. Rooms are large and comfortable. You'll enjoy spending time in the lobby that features a 12-story high glass-enclosed atrium. Our children love the floating piano – a baby grand that is adrift on an island in the middle of a lagoon that lies in the center of the bar.

J.W. Marriott, 1331 Pennsylvania Avenue NW, 800/228-9290 or 202/393-2000, Fax 202/626-6991, www.marriotthotels.com. 772 units, Rates: $159 for two double beds, but ask for specials that could bring the price down to $89, Restaurant: Lots of choice – three hotel restaurants and a food court – the hotel is connected to a mall, Babysitting: yes, check with the concierge. Metro: Metro Center.

We have attended many business and political meetings here – some were huge events. Yet, it serves families well, too. There is an indoor pool, fitness center and game room. You are only two blocks from the White House and near to the Convention Center.

Expensive/Moderate

Hotel Washington, 515 15th Street NW, 800/424-9540, Fax 202/638-1595, 350 guestrooms, Babysitting: can make arrangements Rates: Ask for family special for $100 per night, otherwise $190 to $250), Restaurant: Two Continents (lobby level breakfast and lunch buffet, to floor for dinner) and Sky Terrace (open May through October for dinner) Metro: Farragut North.

Dinner on the rooftop is divine, with a spectacular view of the U.S. Treasury Building and the White House. Stop here even if you aren't guests. The hotel is refined and elegant. Work out at the fitness center, relax in the sauna and get your hair done for a night out on the town at the hotel's salon.

Moderate

Renaissance Washington, D.C., Hotel, 999 9th Street NW, 800/228-9898 or 202/898-9000, Fax 202/789-4213, www.Renaissancehotels.com. 801 unites (Convention Center and MCI Center, Babysitting: can make arrangements, Rates: $129 and up for two double beds, some connecting rooms – double the price – and suites, with a pull-out coach – at $320, Restaurant: The Florentine (breakfast, lunch, dinner),Caracella and Plaza Gourmet (a deli, great sandwiches to go), Metro: Metro C enter or Gallery Place.

Lovely mega-size hotel, with a fitness center, just steps away from Chinatown and the Convention and MCI Centers. Enjoy the fitness center and indoor pool.

Governor's House Hotel, 17th Street and Rhode Island Avenue NW 202/ 296-2100, 146 guestrooms, Babysitting: yes, call in advance, Rates: range from a low of $99 to $209, Restaurant: breakfast, lunch and dinner, Metro: Farragut North.

Barbara used to stay sometimes when she came in from Chicago on business. So did Michael even longer ago when he visited Washington with his family. The staff is still very friendly. There is an outdoor pool and fitness center, but you also have access to the YMCA across the street. Our children love the Y. The pool is Olympic size (children are allowed in only on weekends) and there is a climbing wall.

Lincoln Suites, 1823 L Street NW, 800/424-2970 or 202/223-4320, Fax 202/223-8546, www.lincolnhotels.com. 99 studio suites, Babysitting: no, Restaurant: Samantha's and Beatrice, Rates: $139-$189, Metro: Farragut North or Farragut West (orange and blue lines)

Many of the suites have full kitchens, the others have microwaves and refrigerators. The location – right downtown, about five blocks from the White House. The look – cool and hip. Enjoy the complimentary milk and cookies in the evening. One of the best moderately priced deals in town.

Morrison-Clark Inn, Massachusetts Avenue NW, 800/332-7898, 202/ 898-1200, Fax 202/289-8567, www.morrisonclark.com. Rates: $150-$300, but ask for their different rate plans. Restaurant: Metro: Metro Center, but far enough away to need a taxi.

So charming, the Morrison-Clark Inn once was two separate townhouses. Some rooms feature fireplaces, others are transformed carriage houses. Eat a continental breakfast in the lovely dining area. The restaurant is nationally acclaimed and features southern cooking, with general American fare, as well. You are in walking distance to Ford's Theater and the MCI Center, but it may be a bit of a hike for young ones.

Inexpensive

Hotel Harrington, 436 11th Avenue NW (corner of 11th and E Streets NW), 202/628-8140 or 800/424-8532, Fax 202/347-3924, www.hotel-harrington.com.254 guest rooms, 26 deluxe family rooms, Babysitting: no, Rates: family rate $95, deluxe family room $155, Restaurant: three restaurants take care of breakfast, lunch and dinner, Metro: Metro Center.

Dare we say, best deal in town? Hotel Harrington is a 1/2 block from

Pennsylvania Ave between the White House and Capitol. The hotel is still owned and operated by its founding families, after 88 years!

Red Roof Inn, 500 H Street NW, 800/843-7663, 202/289-5959, www.redroof.com. 195 guestrooms, Babysitting: no, Rates: around $100. Restaurant: breakfast and lunch. Metro: Gallery Place.

Right, smack in the middle of Chinatown. The Red Roof Inn's rooms are more spacious than expected. There also is a washer-dryer and a small health club.

DUPONT CIRCLE/FOGGY BOTTOM

Very Expensive

Topaz Hotel, 1733 N Street NW, 202/393-3000, www.topazhotel.com. 90 guestrooms, Babysitting: can make arrangements, Rate: $139-$259, (Their website notes that they will match any room rate you may find for their hotel listed on another website.) Restaurant: Topaz Bar (weekends breakfast and dinner only, weekdays breakfast, lunch and dinner), Metro: Dupont Circle

Quaint and cozy, the Canterbury is where we spent our wedding night. It once was Teddy Roosevelt's private residence. Now the Canterbury has been transformed into the Topaz, a New Age hotel in downtown D.C. Whoa! Each room comes with "exotic" teas and automatic teapot, daily horoscope, power bars and Aveda bath products. The Big Sur-lover in us says way to go. Check out their package deals: The Big Rub: For $299 you get overnight accommodations, a his and her massage, aromatherapy oils, tranquility CD and energy elixir. The Celestial Sensation package ($255) includes a psychic reading and tickets to the planetarium at Air and Space. Better yet, pets welcome!!

Washington Hilton & Towers, 1919 Connecticut Avenue NW, 202/483-3000, 1,100 guestrooms, Rates: $165 and up, come on the weekend for a deal, Restaurant: Five restaurants take care of all your eating needs, Metro: Dupont Circle.

Home of big, big, big political events and the spot where John Hinkley Jr. attempted to assassinate President Reagan; there's a lot going on at this Hilton. If you like small, cozy, private hotels – think again. There are over 1,000 rooms here! One of the best aspects of this Hilton: the huge outdoor pool and children's pool. Tennis courts and health club will keep you in shape. The rooms and lobby are quite contemporary and the view from the fifth floor up is stunning.

Moderate/Expensive

Doubletree Guest Suites, 801 New Hampshire Avenue NW, 202/785-2000 Fax 785-9485, www.hilton.com. 105 suites, Babysitting: can make arrangements, Rates: $144, with Friday check-in, Restaurant: room service only for breakfast and dinner, Metro: Foggy Bottom.

All suites have a full kitchen, microwave and living room with a pullout bed and separate bedroom. There are several connecting rooms for families. Enjoy the pool.

Carlyle Suites, 1731 New Hampshire Avenue NW, 202/234-3200, Fax 202/387-0085, www.carlylesuites.com. 170 suites, Babysitting: no Rates: $129 to $200 (2 queens, full kitchen), Children under 18 stay free, Restaurant: breakfast, lunch, dinner, Metro: Dupont Circle (Q Street exit).

Art deco in the midst of Dupont Circle. This is a great location – near a Metro and all the shops, bookstores, cafes of Dupont Circle.

Radisson Barcelo Hotel, 2121 P Street NW, 800/333-3333, 300 guest rooms, Rates: $155-$189, but ask for weekend and summer specials, Restaurant: Gabriel, features Spanish cuisine and excellent tapas, **Metro:** Dupont Circle (red line)

Huge rooms make family living easy. You also will love the outside pool set in a garden.

Moderate

The George Washington University Inn, 824 New Hampshire Avenue NW, 800/426-4455, 202/337-6620, Babysitting: no, but may be able to make arrangements, Restaurant: no restaurant, but complimentary breakfast available, Rates: $99 to $135, but a summer special can get you as low as $74, Metro: Foggy Bottom.

This charming hotel once was an apartment building. George Washington University purchased it just a few years ago and renovated.

GEORGETOWN

Very Expensive

Four Seasons Hotel, 2800 Pennsylvania Ave NW, 202/342-0444, Fax (202) 342-1673, www.fourseasons.com/washington. 259 units, Babysitting: yes, Rates: $335-$1,575 Restaurant: Seasons (breakfast, lunch, dinner) and Garden Terrace Lounge (lunch, afternoon tea, and Sunday brunch), Metro: there is no Metro serving Georgetown, yet.

You or your children couldn't ask for more! Although staying here for a week is commiserate with paying for a private high school education in Washington, the Four Seasons knows how to take care of visitors.

Of course, it is beautifully appointed and the rooms luxurious. Services: everything – full fitness center, spa, limousine service, 24-hour room service. A real surprise to us, however, is their emphasis on children. The hotel's V.I.C. (Very Important Children) program may be a bow to the pampered children of the rich and famous, but it's a wonderful notion for all children. Children get milk and cookies, balloons, games and magazines and teddy bears. They are given flotation devices and toys to use at the pool. Have baby, will travel to the Four Seasons sans diaper bag. They have it all: crib, bottle and warmer, diapers, high chair and floor mat. Unbelievable.

Moderate

Georgetown Suites, 1000 29th Street NW, 800/348-7203, 78 suites, Babysitting: no, Rates: $99 to $139, Restaurant: No, but serves continental breakfast, Metro: Georgetown does not yet have a Metro stop.

This is an all-suite hotel. Each unit has a living room, dining room and kitchen. A washer-dryer also is available. Work out at the fitness center and stroll through lovely Georgetown during the evenings.

Holiday Inn Georgetown, 2101 Wisconsin Avenue NW, 202/338-4600, FAX 338-4458, www.holidayinn.com. 296 guestrooms, Babysitting: no Rates: $119 to $130, but ask about summer deal that could bring the price down, Restaurant: breakfast, lunch, dinner, Metro: There is no Metro in Georgetown.

Slightly off the beaten track, but just blocks from the hub-bub of Georgetown. You can walk to M Street and take the bus to the monuments and the Mall or metro stop or take cab to your destination. Enjoy the outdoor pool and fitness center. And, make sure to ask about the Holiday Inn's Family Fun Package, which guarantees your family a free breakfast every day (up to $10 per person) and other goodies.

CLEVELAND PARK/WOODLEY PARK

Expensive/Moderate

Omni Shoreham Hotel, 2500 Calvert Street NW, 800/THE-OMNI or 202/234-0700, Fax 202/756-5145, www.omnihotels.com. 825 guestrooms, Babysitting: yes, Rates: $139 an up, Restaurant: Roberts, open from 6:30am to 10:30pm, Metro: Woodley Park-Zoo.

This is a fun place to stay. The outdoor pool is great. Rooms are more than comfortable. You are right near the National Zoo, a metro and Rock Creek Park, for that early morning run. There is a health club ($7 a day). The Omni Shoreham also created the Omni Kids Program, with all sorts of age-appropriate toys and surprises for children from birth to 12.

Inexpensive/Moderate

Connecticut Avenue Days Inn, 4400 Connecticut Avenue NW, 202/244-5600, Fax 202/244-6794, www.daysinn/washingtondc.com. 155 guestrooms, Babysitting: no, Rates: $99 to $119 Restaurant: Tesoro, serves lunch and dinner, Metro: Van Ness

Despise the congestion of downtown areas? Prefer to be a bit away from the maddening crowd? Here's a good place for you. The newly renovated Connecticut Avenue Days Inn is away from the hectic pace of Capitol Hill, downtown and Georgetown, but only by a metro stop. It is located past the

National Zoo and just one stop past Cleveland Park on the Metro. This Days Inn is the proud winner of Five Sunbursts, the highest honor given by the Days Inn corporation.

INDEX

Things Change!

Phone numbers, prices, addresses, quality of food, etc, all change. If you come across any new information, we'd appreciate hearing from you. No item is too small! Drop us an email note at: jopenroad@aol.com, or write us at:

Washington, DC with Kids
Open Road Publishing, P.O. Box 284
Cold Spring Harbor, NY 11724

Travel Notes

Travel Notes

Travel Notes

Travel Notes

Open Road Publishing

U.S.
America's Cheap Sleeps, $14.95
America's Most Charming Towns &
   Villages, $16.95
Arizona Guide, $16.95
Boston Guide, $13.95
California Wine Country Guide, $12.95
Colorado Guide, $16.95
Hawaii Guide, $18.95
Las Vegas Guide, $15.95
Las Vegas With Kids, $14.95
National Parks With Kids, $14.95
New Mexico Guide, $16.95
San Francisco Guide, $16.95
Southern California Guide, $18.95
Spa Guide, $14.95
Texas Guide, $16.95
Utah Guide, $16.95
Vermont Guide, $16.95
Walt Disney World Guide, $14.95
Washington, DC with Kids, $14.95

Middle East/Africa
Egypt Guide, $17.95
Kenya Guide, $18.95

Eating & Drinking on the Open Road
Eating & Drinking in Paris, $9.95
Eating & Drinking in Italy, $9.95
Eating & Drinking in Spain, $9.95
Eating & Drinking in Latin America, $9.95

Latin America & Caribbean
Bahamas Guide, $13.95
Belize Guide, $16.95
Bermuda Guide, $14.95
Caribbean Guide, $21.95
Caribbean With Kids, $14.95
Central America Guide, $21.95
Chile Guide, $18.95
Costa Rica Guide, $17.95
Ecuador & Galapagos Islands Guide, $17.95
Guatemala Guide, $18.95
Honduras Guide, $16.95

Europe
Czech & Slovak Republics Guide, $18.95
Greek Islands Guide, $16.95
Holland Guide, $17.95
Ireland Guide, $18.95
Italy Guide, $21.95
Italy With Kids, $14.95
London Guide, $14.95
Moscow Guide, $16.95
Paris with Kids, $14.95
Prague Guide, $14.95
Rome Guide, $14.95
Scotland Guide, $17.95
Spain Guide, $18.95
Turkey Guide, $19.95

Asia
China Guide, $21.95
Japan Guide, $21.95
Philippines Guide, $18.95
Tahiti & French Polynesia Guide, $19.95
Tokyo Guide, $13.95
Thailand Guide, $18.95

For US orders, include $5.00 for postage and handling for the first book ordered; for each additional book, add $1.00. Orders outside US, inquire first about shipping charges (money order payable in US dollars on US banks only for overseas shipments). Send to:
   Open Road Publishing, PO Box 284, Cold Spring Harbor, NY 11724